IMAGES OF ASIA

Japanese Cinema: An Introduction

# TITLES IN THE SERIES

At the Chinese Table
T. C. LAI

Balinese Paintings (2nd ed.)
A. A. M. DJELANTIK

Bamboo and Rattan:
Traditional Use and Beliefs
JACQUELINE M. PIPER

The Birds of Java and Bali
derek holmes and
STEPHEN NASH

The Birds of Sumatra and Kalimantan
derek holmes and
STEPHEN NASH

Borobudur (2nd ed.)
JACQUES DUMARÇAY

Chinese Almanacs
RICHARD J. SMITH

Chinese Bridges
RONALD G. KNAPP

Chinese Classical Furniture
GRACE WU BRUCE

The Chinese House: Craft, Symbol,
and the Folk Tradition
RONALD G. KNAPP

Chinese Jade
JOAN HARTMAN-GOLDSMITH

Chinese Painting
T. C. LAI

Chinese Snuff Bottles
ROBERT KLEINER

Chinese Tomb Figurines
ANN PALUDAN

Early Maps of South-East Asia (2nd ed.)
R. T. FELL

The House in South-East Asia
JACQUES DUMARÇAY

Images of the Buddha in Thailand
DOROTHY H. FICKLE

Indonesian Batik: Processes, Patterns
and Places
SYLVIA FRASER-LU

Japanese Cinema: An Introduction
DONALD RICHIE

Korean Musical Instruments
KEITH HOWARD

Korean Painting
KEITH PRATT

The Kris: Mystic Weapon of the
Malay World (2nd ed.)
EDWARD FREY

Life in the Javanese Kraton
AART VAN BEEK

Macau
CESAR GUILLEN-NUÑEZ

Mammals of South-East Asia (2nd ed.)
EARL OF CRANBROOK

Mandarin Squares: Mandarins and
their Insignia
VALERY M. GARRETT

The Ming Tombs
ANN PALUDAN

Musical Instruments of South-East
Asia
ERIC TAYLOR

Old Bangkok
MICHAEL SMITHIES

Old Manila
RAMÓN MA. ZARAGOZA

Old Penang
SARNIA HAYES HOYT

Old Shanghai
BETTY PEH-T'I WEI

Old Singapore
MAYA JAYAPAL

Sarawak Crafts: Methods, Materials,
and Motifs
HEIDI MUNAN

Silverware of South-East Asia
SYLVIA FRASER-LU

Songbirds in Singapore: The Growth
of a Pastime
LESLEY LAYTON

Traditional Chinese Clothing in
Hong Kong and South China
1840–1980
VALERY M. GARRETT

*Series Editors, China Titles:*
## NIGEL CAMERON, SYLVIA FRASER-LU

# Japanese Cinema
*An Introduction*

DONALD RICHIE

HONG KONG
OXFORD UNIVERSITY PRESS
OXFORD   NEW YORK

Oxford University Press

Oxford   New York
Athens   Auckland   Bangkok   Bombay
Calcutta   Cape Town   Dar es Salaam   Delhi
Florence   Hong Kong   Istanbul   Karachi
Kuala Lumpur   Madras   Madrid   Melbourne
Mexico City   Nairobi   Paris   Singapore
Taipei   Tokyo   Toronto

and associated companies in
Berlin   Ibadan

Oxford is a trade mark of Oxford University Press

First published 1990
This impression (lowest digit)
3  5  7  9  11  12  10  8  6  4

Published in the United States
by Oxford University Press, New York

British Library Cataloguing in Publication Data

Richie, Donald 1924–
Japanese cinema: an introduction. — (Images of Asia)
1. Japanese cinema films, history
I. Title   II. Series
791.43′0952
ISBN 0-19-584950-7

Library of Congress Cataloging-in-Publication Data

Richie, Donald, 1924–
Japanese cinema : an introduction / Donald Richie.
p.    cm. — (Images of Asia)
Includes bibliographical references.
ISBN 0-19-584950-7
1. Motion pictures — Japan — History.   I. Title.   II. Series.
PN1993.5.J3R474   1990
791.43′0952—dc20      89-29893
CIP

Printed in Hong Kong
Published by Oxford University Press (China) Ltd
18/F Warwick House, Taikoo Place, 979 King's Road,
Quarry Bay, Hong Kong

For Earle Ernst

We are Japanese, so
we should make Japanese
things.[1]

*Ozu Yasujiro*

# Preface

THE history of the cinema in Japan is not so very different from its history in other countries. None the less, when faced with the product of a culture so disparate from our own, we can and often do misinterpret. Our appreciation of a Japanese film may be only partial because we are unaware of the cultural assumptions made by the director.

This introduction to Japanese cinema attempts to define some of these assumptions within a brief history of Japanese film. At the same time it indicates how early Japanese cinema accommodated influences from elsewhere and how Japanese film, like much of Japanese contemporary culture, became an amalgam of the native and the foreign, welded into a new entity.

A short work, this introduction sacrifices much else. Some directors, many films, the vagaries of the industry — all of this has been left out. It can, however, be found in other writings, a number of which are included in the bibliography.

Once again I wish to acknowledge the assistance given me by the Kawakita Memorial Film Institute: for the opportunities to review films and all the monochrome stills in this volume. The Japan Foundation also allowed me to view films, and the colour stills are from the Art Theatre Guild of Japan, the Shibata Organization, Oshima Nagisa, Morita Yoshimitsu, Itami Juzo, Teshigahara Hiroshi, and Yanagimachi Mitsuo; to all these institutions and individuals I am most grateful. I also remain, for many reasons, grateful to Frank Korn.

Finally, a note on Japanese names. In accordance with

current practice, the Japanese order whereby the family name precedes the given name is followed. As is common practice in non-specialist publications, no diacritical marks are used in the romanization of Japanese names, terms and film titles.

*Tokyo, 1989*                                              DONALD RICHIE

# Contents

| | | |
|---|---|---:|
| | *Preface* | *vii* |
| 1 | From the Beginnings to the Early 1920s | 1 |
| 2 | From 1923 to the Late 1930s | 17 |
| 3 | The 1940s and the 1950s | 37 |
| 4 | From the 1960s to the 1980s | 64 |
| | *Notes* | 86 |
| | *Glossary* | 89 |
| | *Bibliography* | 92 |
| | *Index* | 95 |

# From the Beginnings to the Early 1920s

THE latter half of the nineteenth century was, in Japan even more than elsewhere, an era of expansion. After nearly three hundred years of self-imposed seclusion, Japan had reluctantly opened its doors to the rest of the world and begun that programme of modernization which continues to this day.

Among the modernities imported was that newest of Western wonders, the motion picture, and its popularity was instantaneous. In 1897 the Cinématograph Lumière and the Edison Vitascope made their Osaka débuts within a week of each other, and in the following months both were playing in Tokyo as well. Before the end of the year dignity had been conferred on the new entertainment by a showing at the Kabuki-za, graced by the presence of the Crown Prince.

From the first, however, foreign films were shown in a manner that conformed to Japanese audiences' habits of viewing, as well as to traditional structural premises and methods of narration, all of which differed from those in other parts of the world.

An indication of how viewing habits influenced programming can be seen in the way in which early cinema was shown. Since the public was used to lengthy traditional theatre, several short imported films of the period would be put together to form unusually long programmes. These were also often repeated, thus making the programmes even longer. The novelist Tanizaki Jun'ichiro writes of the films he saw around 1898, when he was about ten years old: 'The ends of the reel would be joined together so that the same scene could be projected over and over. I can still remember, endlessly repeated, high waves rolling in on a shore somewhere, breaking, and then receding, and of a lone dog playing there, now pursuing, now being pursued by the retreating and advancing waters.'[2]

Also, since the mechanics of presentation were often a part of the entertainment in traditional Japanese theatre, the spectators' interest in the projector was initially almost as great as in what was being projected. There are reports of showings where the entrepreneur put the machine at the right side of the stage and the screen at the left. Few could see the image properly but all had a full view of the projector and its crew in action. It was a large crew because the dignity of the newly imported and expensive contrivance seemed to demand ample ministration. Sometimes the crew numbered more than ten, including a boy to fan the experts gathered about the hot machine.

Early film performances in Japan were often, in this sense, theatrical because, from the first, the cinema was regarded as an extension of the stage, a new kind of drama, and not as in the West a new kind of photography. There was thus ample reason to incorporate elements from the traditional theatre into early film performances, and into early productions as well. There was also reason, initially at any rate, to disregard any claims for realism, which in the West was considered essential in a photograph, be it still or moving.

An example of traditional theatrical influence on Japanese film was the assumption that all drama had to be 'presented'. While dramatic situations might be represented on the stage, they were also to be presented simultaneously by an authoritative voice. The Noh play has its chorus, the Bunraku doll-drama its *joruri* singer, and the

Kabuki its *gidayu* chanter. These voices give an often redundant description of the action, offer an explanation of motive, and usually tender a moralistic commentary.

All these forms of theatre — and to their number might be added the *kodan* history-story tellers, the comic *rakugo* — share the assumption that the telling of the story is as interesting as its enactment. A story can thus be fragmented, can even be without a logic of its own, since it is the duty of the presenting voice to make it coherent, moving and memorable.

In a Japanese film this voice became the *benshi*, a compère who, like the earlier lantern-slide commentator from which he partially derived, explained, commented upon, and made the parts into a coherent whole. This authoritative voice was necessary because imported films were composed of foreign scenes, and these new sights had to be interpreted, commented upon, and translated into terms comprehensible to the audience.

The *benshi* also fulfilled another, equally important, function — that of satisfying theatrical expectations. As the critic Yoshida Chieo has written: 'In the Bunraku, the doll does the acting ... while what we might call the "characterization" is delivered by the narrator, located in the extreme corner of the stage ... in cinematic terms, the image on the screen is the puppet and the *benshi* is the narrator.'[3]

As a result *benshi* performances were impressive. The banging of the wooden clappers heard in Kabuki would hush the crowd and usher in the *benshi*, who was often attired in a formal frock coat. He would launch into a lengthy introduction of the film, as well as of himself, and it was only after these various advertisements that the show could start. Accompanied by a piano, violin or cornet, and — a Japanese contribution — *samisen*, the *benshi*, often using the somewhat vocal style of the didactic *kodan* chanter, would begin his explication.

Though the *benshi* were provided (after 1910) with dialogue scripts, there are few records of their use. Rather, as befitted a privileged person, the *benshi* made the films his own, often to the extent that a picture compèred by one *benshi* was quite different from the same movie compered by another. Despite this, or perhaps precisely because of this, the *benshi* were extremely popular. One attended a showing as much to hear the narrator as to see the film. The name of the *benshi* was often more prominent on the poster than that of the picture he was accompanying, and a good *benshi* received a large portion of a theatre's takings.

The *benshi* was not without rivals, however. One was the *kagezerifu* or 'shadow-speech' actor who stood behind the screen, modestly dubbing a presumed dialogue — a technique derived from early experiments where film and live drama were combined to form a hybrid entertainment. Another was the *kowairo* or 'voice colourer', a self-effacing narrator who limited his efforts to presenting the presumed dialogue of the characters on the screen. However, neither rival was to prove a lasting threat to the *benshi*. Indeed, he made use of their techniques in perfecting a presentation that, being non-realistic, was even more resoundingly Japanese.

For these reasons the *benshi* flourished, and continued to do so for nearly thirty years, until the advent of the sound film. To this day his influence is still manifest in the superfluous explanation often encountered in Japanese films, the presentation rather than the representation of an emotion, and the sudden, direct commentary — for example, that disembodied voice in the middle of Kurosawa's *Ikiru*. In addition, the common voice-over which detaches audiences from emotion, the spoken meditation which creates the elegiac mood, the pronouncement which lends a feeling of inevitability — all these are also part of the legacy of the *benshi*.

When Japan began to make its own films, an early criticism was that they were mere illustrations for the *benshi*. And so they were. *Benshi* work best with stage-like cinema: actors distant from the camera, long takes, lack of any editing except in a simple connective sense — these indeed suited the *benshi* better than the more overtly 'cinematic'.

Not surprisingly all the earliest Japanese productions were of theatrical events: geisha doing classical dances, a famous Kabuki actor in a famous scene from a famous Kabuki; portions of popular *shimpa* melodramas; dance-like sword fights. However, while audiences were enjoying these early productions, they were also seeing more sophisticated fare from abroad, and noticing the differences.

A member of such an audience was Ozu Yasujiro, later to become one of Japan's finest directors. 'I used to open the door of the movie theatre and smell the stale air,' he recalled. 'It always gave me a headache but I couldn't stay away. Film had a magical hold on me. . . . The movies at that time did nothing more than follow the plot . . . but then an American film, *Civilization* by Thomas Ince, was shown . . . that was when I decided I wanted to be a film director.'[4] Though he was speaking of a slightly later period (the Ince picture was released in 1916) and of one of the most plot-bound of early American films, Ozu was obviously impressed by its intricacy and sophistication, so different from simple and almost static Japanese films.

One reason why early Japanese films seem so uncomplicated, apart from their simple presentation of story, is

screen and into an illusion of space; one looks *at* the screen. And the result is not only the painterly scenes of Mizoguchi and the graphic layouts of Ichikawa Kon, but also the flat compositions of directors otherwise as disparate as Ito Daisuke, Ozu, Kurosawa and Oshima Nagisa, in which 'the playing area is the screen itself'.[6]

In Japanese films the compositions carry more than their simple narrative message — they speak of and for themselves. Their reason for being is, partially at least, to display their own aesthetic. For that reason an aesthetically patterned narrative is sometimes preferred to one that is more logical.

Since neither physical nor psychological depth is sought, the kind of narrative tightness so prized in the West is not found in Japanese films. The idea that each unit or scene should push the story through to its conclusion is not one to which Japanese literature, drama or film subscribes. Rather, separate scenes can be devoted to separate events: the flights of the lovers, the soliloquy, the recognition scene, and so on. These might halt the narrative but they also contain, for a Japanese audience, moments of beauty, contemplation, familiarity, which it finds appropriate and satisfying. Telling a story realistically, scene by scene, is not the most suitable mode of presentation when there is more than mere story to the narrative.

Traditionally there are a number of linear possibilities. One might be the story, but the others are non-narrative: compositional links, associative editing, an unstated subject, and so on. Indeed, sometimes a knowledge of the story is assumed — as in all versions of *The Loyal Forty-seven Ronin* [*Chushingura*], some 84 in all beginning in 1911 — so that it all but disappears, leaving a series of scenes threaded on an invisible narrative. Sometimes various scenes suggest not so much a story as a relationship, of one character to another, or of a character to his or her environment.

Another problem to the Western viewer (who will have found these films slow, vague, meandering and hard to follow) is that the Japanese retain a high regard for convention and a relatively low regard for originality. This means that clichés are endlessly repeated and stereotypes welcomed. Despite the many exceptions to this generalization there remains a tradition which insists upon such invariables. The Japanese film is filled with them: falling cherry blossoms for doomed lovers, dark glasses for bad foreigners.... The Western film is, to be sure, equally replete with clichés and stereotypes, but whereas the Japanese accept these as a matter of form, the Western audience tends to decry them.

Though Japanese films remain text-bound, narrative logic is not always deemed structurally necessary. In Japanese writing, for example, particularly in essay writing, it is not only acceptable but even elegant to jump about from one subject to another. Likewise, in films, variety is often preferred to logic. In both writing and on the screen transitional passages which the West would find structurally indispensable are often missing.

At the same time, perhaps consequently, there is a certain 'eventlessness' in Japanese narrative. Things do not seem to happen with the finality that they do in the dramatic West. Irrelevant or tangential events are considered equal to those of the story itself, and there is small attempt to structure a convincing simulacrum of what in the West is called life. What the Japanese conceive of as life is, however, convincingly conveyed by these various treatments of space and time, movement and narrative, all of which reflect Japanese perceptions of life, and conceptions of how art should present experience.

The history of Japanese cinema is in part the story of the survival of this style, ever less evident as the decades pass but never, even in the late 1980s, altogether gone. At the same time this history is an account of the ways in which Western cinematic innovations were incorporated, to the point where Japanese film style became 'international'. This internationalism is not completely authentic, however, as most Japanese films are coloured by the continuing assumptions of the director and by the ingrained expectations of the spectators.

The older conventions were popularly seen in the films made by Japan's first 'name' director, Makino Shozo (with Japan's first 'star', the actor Onoe Matsunosuke). These pictures emerge as mainly photographed stage plays, the stationary camera at some distance from the actors, an entire scene played out in one long take. There are no close-ups and the acting is best described as theatrical. All of these conventions were found unexceptionable by the Japanese audience. Artistic conventions had created an approximation of perceived reality.

Not all of this audience, however, was so complacent. There was a small segment which criticized this carrying over of older aesthetic precepts into the new art of the cinema. These critics were not ordinary movie-goers. They were, by and large, those writers, directors and actors who were already in revolt against the commercial theatre of the period and who were now turning their attention to film.

This theatre divided drama into two categories: the *kyuha* (old school), meaning mainly Kabuki; and *shimpa* (new school), modern stories in contemporary settings. The new drama now advocated was named Shingeki and was directly related to the realist 'reformation' taking place in Western theatre. The plays of Ibsen, Chekhov and

Gorky were being seen in Japan, and young directors and writers wanted to pursue this new apparent realism.

To the Japanese, the Western idea of realism was something truly new. All early Japanese dramatic forms had assumed the necessity of an artificial structure through which mediation was possible. So had Japanese culture in general: the wilderness was natural only after it had been shaped and presented as a Japanese garden; flowers were considered living (*ikebana*) only after having been cut and arranged for viewing. Life was thus dramatically lifelike only after having been explained and commented upon.

Shingeki insisted otherwise: life must be presented as it appears. That the new drama itself was shortly to become as presentational as Kabuki through a rigid theatrical style called 'realistic' is revealing but irrelevant here. The influence of the Shingeki reform assured that dramatic presentation was, to a degree, revolutionized.

In film this meant that foreign techniques (close-ups, shorter takes, logical narrative) began to be employed for functions similar to those in Western cinema. At the same time, however, these elements of a foreign style were typically altered.

In the first Shingeki-influenced picture, a 1914 adaptation of a Tolstoy story, *Katusha* (Kachusha), directed by Hosoyama Kiyomatsu, authentic Russian gowns were used, but on female impersonators. A later Tolstoy adaptation, *Living Corpse* (Ikeru shikabane, 1917), directed by Tanaka Eizo, showed a dramatically motivated close-up but, typically, used it in a traditionally Japanese manner.

In the West it is believed that a close-up ensures empathy. The convention is that we feel as strongly as our heroine does during those moments when we see her enormous image on the screen. Tanaka, however, uses the close-up (actually a bust-shot) to show her merely engaged in opening the letter containing the bad news. For the weeping scene itself, Tanaka — in direct opposition to accepted Western practice — moves back to long shot. In so doing he sacrifices any notion of emotional empathy. At the same time, however, he can better comment upon his scene in a more Japanese manner: there she stands, alone, under a lowering sky, by the single tree as solitary as herself.

If the Western audience perceived emotion through intimacy with a face, the Japanese perceived it through forms set in their environment, seen through long shots, long takes and the pathetic fallacy.

Representative of the new producer-directors coming from Shingeki was Kaeriyama Norimasa, who proclaimed in 1917 that he was going 'to make films in the American style', by which he meant more realistic acting styles, a repertoire of long, medium, and close-up shots, and some Griffith-like editing. He was also to use actresses for the female parts, something vigorously opposed by the female-impersonator guilds.

The first of these actresses was Hanayagi Harumi in *Glow of Life* (Sei no kagayaki, 1918). She was not, however, popular, women on the screen being too much of a novelty. This fact and the animosity of the *benshi*, angry at being deprived of prerogatives by the new representational films, ensured that this and other early Shingeki-influenced films were not given adequate distribution.

Despite this initial lack of success further attempts were made, notably by Osanai Kaoru, one of the founders of Shingeki itself. The finest of his films was *Souls on the Road* (Rojo no reikon, 1921). Co-directed with Murata Minoru who had worked with Kaeriyama, it was the picture which for many marks the true beginning of the Japanese cinema.

*Souls on the Road* (Rojo no reikon, 1921, Osanai Kaoru and Murata Minoru)
Hisamatsu Mikio, Suzuki Denmei, Sawamura Haruko

*Crossroads* (Jujiro, 1928, Kinugasa Teinosuke)
Bando Junnosuke, Chihaya Akiko

This film is composed (in the Griffith manner) of several parallel stories. One is taken from Shingeki's favourite author, Maxim Gorky, about two ex-convicts trying to go straight, and another from a *shimpa* play (based on a drama by Wilhelm Schmidtbonn) about the return home of the contrite wastrel. Sources East and West meet in these stories, as do their methods of treatment. This is indeed the first film to illustrate the hybrid nature of the Japanese cinematic style and to indicate how accommodations may be turned into strengths.

Superficially the picture displays Western style to an extreme. It opens and closes with a literary quotation (a passage from *The Lower Depths*); there is indeed a plethora of language: 127 titles in an 80-minute film, many more than usual in a film of this period. The young daughter of the house, hair in long ringlets, is dressed to look like Mary Pickford and acts like her. The action takes place on Christmas Eve, an 'exotic' festival to the Japanese. There are all sorts of devices such as wipes, fades, dissolves and irises, noticeable intercutting among the stories (no matter that such *Intolerance*-like editing is to the Western eye in no way appropriate to the slightness of the domestic tragedies involved), as well as a number of close-ups (bust-shots).

The close-ups are not used, however, for moments of high drama; for these the camera pulls back to reveal a family tableau. Nor is the intercutting used to intensify the excitement of synchronous happenings. Indeed, there is no attempt to create a sense of the simultaneous as each story stops abruptly as soon as it is not pursued on the screen. When we return to it this story is at the point where we left it and we then pick up its thread. In *Souls on the Road* the 'problem' of lapsed time is not dealt with in the stories or in the editing. In fact it is not perceived as a problem.

The same is true of traditional Japanese dramaturgy. Very little ever happens off stage and there is no strong tradition of informing the audience of what they do not see. Thus it is quite natural for Osanai and Murata to treat time as aesthetically as they treat space. They may have thought of their film as realistic in the Western manner, but it emerges as realistic in a Japanese manner.

Flashbacks are used to both fill out and decorate the narrative. For this reason flashbacks and even flashes into alternative situations (happy scene showing what might have happened if only father had forgiven the erring son, for example) are used for pictorial rather than psychological effect.

Despite its Western look, *Souls on the Road* is very Japanese in that it evidences a 'disruption of narrative linearity', and in any event this narrative is 'only one "voice" in a polyphony that gives equal role to purely spatial manipulations'.[7]

What comes across is the beauty of the patterning, not the power or the pathos of the drama shown on the screen. Empathy is denied: when we see the dark skies and distant fields commenting upon the souls on the road, it is a general statement about homelessness, not an observation on the homelessness of the two ex-convicts. The creation of a mediating atmosphere, one which suggests rather than states, is the true realism of these first serious directors.

The director becomes the mediator between raw emotion and the spectator. This is also true in other countries, but there the demands of an illusionary realism and Western audiences' acceptance of this style rendered the director's role much less visible, except for directors such as Lubitsch and, later, Alfred Hitchcock.

In Japan this was not so. With no 'realism' to distract the

viewer, the mediation of the director himself was quite evident. And this was first seen clearly in the patterned surface of *Souls on the Road*.

## 2
# From 1923 to the Late 1930s

THE great earthquake of 1923 which destroyed so much of Tokyo and Yokohama had a number of positive effects on Japanese cinema. One was that the production of period films (now named *jidaigeki*) was transferred to Kyoto, the old capital, where the necessary 'sets' still existed. The studios in Tokyo were henceforth reserved for *gendaigeki*, as films about contemporary life were now called.

Another result was an even greater popularity of the movies. The disaster had made audiences ready for light, irrelevant entertainment, for a new way to pass the time. Triple features were common and often called upon the services of two *benshi*, one to relieve the other when his voice gave out.

Some criticized the frivolity of this post-earthquake cinema but all attested to its extraordinary popularity. The novelist Nagai Kafu has one of his characters remember being dragged off to the movies shortly after the disaster: 'It was a moving-picture much admired at the time ... turned out to be an adaptation of a Maupassant story. I might have liked the original better. Yet, young and old so delight in moving-pictures that even a person like me sometimes feels inclined to wonder what the conversation might be about.'[8]

The serious viewer may not have had much to choose from among the mindless Japanese melodramas, but he could nevertheless have seen some extraordinary foreign films, since a larger audience meant more imports. The young Kurosawa Akira, then aged 13, kept note of the films he saw in the year following the earthquake, and these included Chaplin's *A Woman of Paris*, Gance's *La Roue*, Ford's *The Iron Horse*, Lang's *Die Nibelungen* and Lubitsch's *The Marriage Circle*.[9]

These pictures not only offered glimpses of distant climes and novel attitudes, but they also demonstrated new methods of presenting and viewing films. Ozu Yasujiro, then just 20, remembered both the Chaplin and the Lubitsch films. 'They were so different ... they had such sophisticated styles that they could express even the smallest nuances of emotion. Before this I had seen nothing but plotted films. I found it fascinating that a film could make me really feel what the characters were feeling ... especially without dialogue, just images.'[10]

Before long Japanese pictures were themselves manifesting deeper influences from foreign films. This was initially most apparent in historical pictures. The reason was that, just as Shingeki had 'reformed' the *gendaigeki*, so now a new period drama, Shinkokugeki (the 'new national drama', a combination as it were of Shingeki and Kabuki) was revitalizing the *jidaigeki* and making use of the more sophisticated techniques now appearing from the West.

The first picture to actually call itself a *shin jidaigeki* (new period film) was Nomura Hotei's *Chuji from Kunisada: A Flock of Wild Geese* (Kunisada Chuji: Kari no mure), but more popular were those of Makino Shozo. He, keeping up with the times, had broken with Matsunosuke; his recipe for film-making had become: 'One, strong plot; two, no inessentials; and, three, continual movement.'[11]

The first of Makino's new period pictures was *The Purple Hood: Woodblock Artist* (Murasaki zukin: ukiyo-e shi, 1923), an action-packed thriller written by Susukita Rokuhei, a young Shingeki playwright whose subsequent scripts would come to define the *jidaigeki* of the 1920s. His major contribution was the application of realist principles to period films. 'I gave Makino a script filled with real violence, real combat scenes, thoroughly realistic. He said it would have to be done with real weapons ... what happiness I felt. Several of the actors were actually hurt by the flailing swords.'[12]

Besides being violently realistic the film also introduced a new kind of hero, a sword-fighting samurai who was also an individual, even a non-conformist. His popularity was such that he was followed by a whole procession of like disaffiliates. Though the stories were often taken from the moralistic and Confucian *kodan* or from popular historical novels, the heroes, brave, athletic and out-spoken, were cut from American cloth and patterned on the cowboys in Westerns.

Japanese audiences flocked to the new *jidaigeki*. They not only liked the blood and gore, but were also excited by the idea that traditional obedience to authority could be questioned. In post-earthquake Japan many traditional social beliefs were being shaken and it appeared that a new era was beginning, one more open, less repressive.

It was not only rebellious samurai who were considered heroic, but also many of those long thought outside the pale of polite society. As early as 1922 Nomura Hotei had written and directed *Jirocho from Shimizu* (Shimizu no Jirocho), a *kodan*-based story about an itinerant *yakuza* gambler. A popular hit, it cleared the way for more of nature's gentlemen. The films were shortly to form a genre, the most famous example of which is Ito Daisuke's three-part *Chuji's Travel Diary* (Chuji tabi nikki, 1927–8).

The most popular of these were based on the novels of Hasegawa Shin, many of which were filmed. In *Tokijiro from Kutsukake* (Kutsukake Tokijiro, 1929), directed by Tsuji Kichiro, the popular Okochi Denjiro played the wandering roughneck who, through a single humanitarian act of saving the wife and child of his rival, attained true self-respect.

Susukita had by this time introduced even further disaffiliates, including the ultimate, the *ronin* or masterless samurai. This hero had no one to whom he could pledge his loyalty. He was free, alone and alienated.

Just as popular and much better as films were the *matatabi-mono* movies of Inagaki Hiroshi, in particular the 1928 *Tenka Taiheiki* (directed with Itami Mansaku). It was Inagaki who made the *jidaigeki* modern: his dialogue-titles used colloquial speech, his heroes were contemporary with their audience. It was he who regarded the *jidaigeki* as '*chonmage o tsuketa gendaigeki* (*gendaigeki* with [samurai] topknots attached)'.[13]

Early *ronin*, those in *Chushingura*, for example, were bound by awful oaths to their rightful lord. The *ronin* in films of the late 1920s were loyal to no one. They not only lacked fedual faith, they seemed to lack any faith at all. They were, indeed, 'nihilistic', a term applied to the very first of them, the 1925 *Orochi*, scripted by Susukita, directed by Futagawa Buntaro and starring Bando Tsumasaburo. Here the *ronin* inhabited a truly meaningless world, one in which no moral order was to be seen, where a man could trust only his feelings.

Among the most powerful of these films was the multi-part *Street of Masterless Samurai* (Roningai, 1928–9), directed by Makino Masahiro, son of Shozo, and scripted by Yamagami Itaro, a story of men who came to question their feudal code and to accept their own humanity. The film exerted a lasting influence on the work of Yamanaka Sadao, Kurosawa, Kobayashi Masaki and later film-makers.

These new realist-action films, in addition to providing nihilistic interest for the new audience, also displayed further innovations learned from the Western cinema. The action was more or less continual, and the camera moved about in a manner not hitherto seen. Shinoda Masahiro, who was later to become a film director, remembered that his elders nicknamed Ito Daisuke, the most action-minded of the new *jidaigeki* directors, 'Ido-daisuki' ('I Love Pan-shots').[14]

It was the young Ito, like Susukita also in his twenties, who is often credited with the cinematic style of the new *jidaigeki*. Originally a stage director, then a script writer, Ito was known as the most socially conscious of the young directors, as well as being especially susceptible to a bloody 'realism'.

In the outspoken *Man-Slashing, Horse-Piercing Sword* (Zanjin zamba ken, 1930) Ito had a disaffiliate *ronin* lead the peasants in violent revolt against the local lord. Such films began to frighten the authorities who moved to censor and eventually to ban them.

Though a part of the popularity of these new *jidaigeki* was their message, they were also liked because they introduced a new kind of popular hero, one quite different from Matsunosuke. These new period-film stars — Okochi Denjiro, Bando Tsumasaburo, Kataoka Chiezo, Tsukigata Ryunosuke — had something of the grace of Fairbanks and the high-minded fairness of Hart. They had kept their swordsman's skills but they were also human.

These new heroes also typified the new film style. Director Itami Mansaku wrote bravely (in wartime 1940) that 'the first thing we learned from American movies was a fast-paced life-style ... the next, a lively manner and a readiness to take decisive action ... we learned to take an affirmative, purposeful, sometimes even combative attitude toward life'.[15]

The new audience admired these new stars. They were

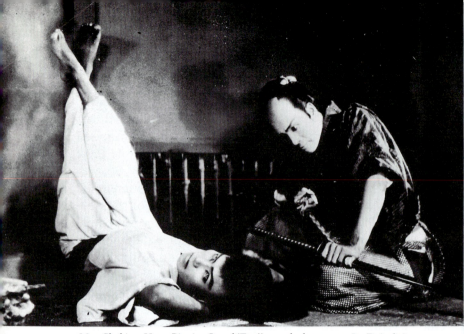

*Man-Slashing, Horse-Piercing Sword* (Zanjin zamba ken, 1930, Ito Daisuke)
Tsukigata Ryunosuke, Amano Junichi

*I Was Born, But . . .* (Umarete wa mita keredo, 1932, Ozu Yasujiro)
Sugawara Hideo, Kato Seiichi, Tokkankozo

also perhaps reassured that though Ito and other *jidaigeki* directors had learned the fast-moving ways of Western cinema, they still retained much of the dramaturgy of the traditional drama. This was particularly evident in the brilliant sword-fight scenes, often played as though on the stage with details shown in sudden close-ups. Visual compositions held the eye and at the same time set the emotional tone of the scene. Like the traditional prints upon which they were sometimes based, these compositions dramatized scene and encapsulated story. As in traditional drama one scene followed the other, impelled not so much by story line as by aesthetic spectacle.

Among the most interesting, if least typical, of these cinematic amalgams were two films by ex-female impersonator turned director, Kinugasa Teinosuke: *A Page Out of Order* (aka *A Page of Madness*, Kurutta ippeiji, 1926), based on a scenario by novelist Kawabata Yasunari, and *Crossroads* (Jujiro, 1928), based on a *kodan* samurai story. Both films are about mental states (distraught wife in asylum in the one and hallucination-prone samurai in the other), a theme not often found in Japanese cinema, but neither delves into psychological motives, then as now so common in Western film.

Such motives have been defined as involving 'psychologically defined individuals who struggle to solve a problem or attain specific goals', and 'the principal causal agent is ... a character endowed with a consistent batch of evident traits'.[16] Japanese film, however, is innocent of all this, and has characters no more dependent upon batches of evident traits than they are upon plot. In the Kinugasa films there are no self-evident personalities, no explanation of various psychological motives and in this sense the pictures are — to a Japanese — quite conservative.

Both *A Page Out of Order* and *Crossroads* are stylistically radical, by comparison not only with Japanese films but with Western films as well. They differ from Japanese film norms in the way in which a chosen reality is expressed. We are directly shown the distorted world that the characters themselves experience. We are invited to share their madness and enjoy the resulting aesthetic tableaux.

*A Page Out of Order* may owe something to *The Cabinet of Dr Caligari*, the 1919 German picture as influential in Japan as elsewhere, but the radical nature of the editing and the lack of logical continuity (as distinct from 'Japanese' continuity in its associative narrative, of which there is a great deal) make it one of the most original of films. At the same time, its expressionistic style — events as experienced by the deranged mind — indicates how well this new stylistic stratagem serves as a voice, as a mediator. Expressionism, by its nature, presents rather than represents and thus has a place as permanent in the Japanese cinema as it has in the German. This expressionism is a continuing style, and can be found in such films as Kurosawa's *Kagemusha* (1980) and *Ran* (1985).

*Crossroads* is, by comparison, the more orthodox film. It is less introverted, more straightforward and, with its Kabuki-like structure of small scenes, more concerned with a surface realism — the cat attracted by blood from the samurai's wound, for example. It is a finely atmospheric *jidaigeki*, though a demanding one.

The financial failure of *A Page Out of Order* may account for the greater orthodoxy of *Crossroads*. In any event, both failed to win general acceptance. The Japanese audience, as much as any other, likes novelty only if it is not too novel. Kinugasa experimented no more, became a successful academic director, and is most remembered for *The Gate of Hell* (Jigokumon, 1952).

While the new *jidaigeki* was concerning itself with

more human samurai, the *gendaigeki* was beginning to investigate the lives of ordinary people. Films about the mysteriously moneyed on the one hand and the picturesquely poverty-stricken on the other no longer appealed to the new audience.

As in most countries, 'life' was late in making a cinematic appearance in Japan. Once it had, however, films about the middle classes (which is what 'life' usually means on the screen) became popular. An early example was Tanaka Eizo's *The Kyoya Collar Shop* (Kyoya erimise, 1922) about the world of small shopkeepers, one which included female impersonators, though this film was the last to use them.

Among the directors best known for films about the middle classes was Shimazu Yasujiro, who had been lighting director on *Souls on the Road*. In 1924 he made a comedy called *Sunday* (Nichiyobi) which was uncommonly perceptive of how people really lived. This was followed by a picture about the rural middle class, *A Village Teacher* (Mura no sensei, 1925). Other directors investigating the new subject-matter were Gosho Heinosuke, in *Townspeople* (Machi no hitobito, 1926), and Ozu Yasujiro who made his first feature about middle-class wage-earners in *The Life of an Office Worker* (Kaishain seikatsu, 1929).

The new *gendaigeki* marked the beginning of genres later to become important to the growing Japanese cinema. From these beginnings came the genre of films about the lower middle class (the neologism for which is *shomingeki*), the serio-comedy of the salaried class (*shoshimingeki*), and the sentimental satire. The last owed its greatest development to Ushihara Kiyohiko, one of the writers of the script of *Souls on the Road*, in which he played the butler.

Japanese films of this period also testified to the continuing influence of Western cinema, in this case American. A series of short (hour-long) pictures from Universal called Bluebird Productions was one of the most powerful sources of American influence. Completely forgotten in their country of origin, these short films had a considerable impact on Japan.

With such titles as *Southern Justice* and *A Kentucky Cinderella*, these pictures were decidedly uncomplicated, with simple plots, determined heroes and 'nature' shots, and they were, from the Japanese point of view, highly realistic. In addition, they displayed an idealistic simplicity which could be instantly grasped and relatively easily copied. The great influence exerted by this series, not at all commensurate with its worth, was later acknowledged by such diverse directors as Ushihara, Kinugasa, Gosho, Ozu and even Ito Daisuke.

What so strongly appealed to these new *gendaigeki* and later directors was the kind of selective 'realism' exhibited by the series. It was not a naturalism which insisted upon including everything, but was 'Japanese' in that it created through stringent selection. Most forms of Japanese art are, in this sense, reductive, and cinema is no exception.

Indeed, many of the recipes which Japanese directors have from time to time given for making good films are reductive by nature. Shimazu Yasujiro is said to have told his pupil Yoshimura Kimisaburo: 'The secret of filmmaking, Yoshimura, is framing.'[17] Likewise, the brilliant young Yamanaka Sadao is said to have had one main theory: 'You establish the position of the camera. After that it is easy.'[18] What both those directors were in their different ways doing was defining through scrupulous selection. Western directors, asked about their secrets, might well have included everything: getting the right script, the proper camera movements, suitable actors.

26

When the film theoretician Sugiyama Heiichi said that 'a film can never *become* reality itself because film always takes place within a frame', he was acknowledging that it is limitations which create the style the Japanese called realist. He went on to suggest why: 'It is restriction of vision which lends things their interest.'[19]

The director who perhaps best typifies this selective and reductive style, both in the late 1920s and later, is Mizoguchi Kenji, of whom Kurosawa once said: 'The great thing [about him] was his tireless effort to imbue every scene with reality.'[20] It was a specific Japanese reality which was sought, and which Kurosawa himself observes, and this search defined the Mizoguchi style.

This style was an amalgam. The most eclectic of directors in his early career, Mizoguchi was at the same time one of the most highly conscious of Japanese traditions. Blending the various influences took, he later said, some time. It was only after 1936 'that I was able finally to learn how to show life as I see it'. What this was, Mizoguchi revealed later: 'You want me to speak of my art? – but that is impossible . . . let us rather say that a man like myself is always tempted by the climate of beauty.'[21] Beauty then is the result of a striving for realism. The realistic consists of a selection of what is considered beautiful, just as in the West the real is often defined by what is not. Mizoguchi's reduction is therefore typical of Japanese style since the will to aestheticize is one of its hallmarks.

In the works of Mizoguchi, perhaps more than in those of any other director, one may also discover a successful marriage of the Western realistic mode and this purely Japanese concern with aesthetics. This is particularly obvious in *Sisters of the Gion* (Gion no shimai, 1936), a film which he himself said marked the beginnings of his mature style. The story of two sisters, one modern, one traditional, seems indeed to mirror the often problematical fusion of East and West which is so well achieved in this picture.

The film also contains in full form one of the means through which Mizoguchi combined a double influence. This is the one-scene, one-shot technique. In the early cinema of most countries this was the most common means of presentation. Early abandoned in the West it continued in Japan. Mizoguchi used it to create a new kind of cinematic tension: the full accoutrements of the Western realist style displayed through the confines of the 'Japanese' single long take. Each scene is allowed to create its own impact; there is no breaking of the scene up into variously positioned shots.

This technique is paramount to the Mizoguchi style. Yoda Yoshikata, who scripted this as well as most of the later films, said: 'The deepest beauty must be recorded with continuous shots . . . I take this single-shot technique into account in all of my scripts.'[22] Its effect has often been commented upon, but its strength was perhaps best described by Shinoda when he compared the long shots of Mizoguchi with the short shots of Ito Daisuke and stressed 'the tremendous increase in emotional impact which [Mizoguchi] gained by exchanging the manipulation of short multiple shots for the objectivity of the long single shot'.[23]

It is precisely this objectivity which impresses, particularly when used in the context of a full range of camera movements and positions, realistic acting, and other Western cinematic means. The chosen reality is rendered with an aesthetic objectivity which compels belief. This continued and restricted view defines not only the beauty but also the truth of the scene, its chosen verisimilitude.

Another example of this Japanese tendency to define through limitations is seen in the work of Ozu Yasujiro, a director who by the early 1930s had successfully fused traditional aesthetic precepts with American influences.

The deliberate limitations of the Ozu style are well known. There are few pans or dollies. There are eventually no fades, no dissolves, techniques which Ozu said were attributes of the camera, not of cinema itself. The viewpoint is usually from a dramatically lowered camera, the equivalent, he once said, of a person sitting on *tatami*. Once the viewpoint is chosen, all actions are confined to the resulting frame, punctuated with but the simple cut. The action is frontal, with people addressing each other 'through' the camera.

Though the young Ozu had been impressed by the plot of *Civilization* and the sophisticated direction of Lubitsch, his own films were restricted to story and anecdote and denied both plot and psychological explanation. He constructed a specifically Japanese geometry on his screen, one designed to contain, indeed to create, the 'realistic' Ozu character. Just as the restriction of the Mizoguchi long-held scene created its own emotional impact, the minimalism of the Ozu technique was in many ways responsible for the memorability of the Ozu character.

*I Was Born, But . . .* (Umarete wa mita keredo, 1932) is often cited as marking the beginning of Ozu's mature style. It is a comedy rendered serious both by its subject (children growing up in an adult world) and by the rigour of its presentation. The late Iwasaki Akira called it 'the first work of social realism in Japanese films.'[24] And so it may be, but it is realism of a peculiarly Japanese variety.

Concerned with patterns and visible structures, Ozu constructed this film from invariable scenes (the house, the vacant lot), from repeated sequences (the boys and their friends), and from various parallel scenes (the railroad crossing). By limiting what is shown Ozu intensifies its effect. Some of the points of the film are made through patterns alone: a dolly (among Ozu's last) along the desks in the boys' school cut against a dolly along the desks in the father's office, camera movements revealing children and adults as nearly identical.

In the early 1930s many young directors were constructing films of a selective verisimilitude. So, indeed, were and are directors around the world. Any film is, by its nature, selective. Only in Japan, however, was the choice so limited, so concise, and so conscious. Only here was realism so openly cropped, cut, moulded.

In *Our Neighbour, Miss Yae* (Tonari no Yae-chan, 1934) Shimazu created a comedy of middle-class life through a balanced series of scenes, parallel action in neighbouring houses, coupled with a radically simplified everydayness — a dramatic geometry just visible under this domestic surface.

A novelettish story about a daughter bringing back together her middle-class estranged parents is turned into an aesthetic experience by Naruse Mikio in his first important film, *Wife, Be Like a Rose* (Tsuma yo bara no yo ni, 1935). Attention is constantly drawn to the patterns of the film, to regular ambiguities in relationship of the characters not only to each other but also to the story itself. The presentation is both assured and self-conscious. If it is reminiscent of Lubitsch it is also suggestive of classical Japanese narrative.

In *A Star Athlete* (Hanagata senshu, 1937), one of a popular series of college-life films, Shimizu Hiroshi created an elaborately patterned film, one in which the construction itself compounds the humour. Style is intimately related to exigencies of the story: certain characters are associated with certain kinds of shots, similar actions are invariably taken in long shots, and pans are revealing.

*Our Neighbour, Miss Yae* (Tonari no Yae-chan, 1934, Shimazu Yasujiro)
Aizome Yumeko, Takasugi Sanae

*Sisters of the Gion* (Gion no shimai, 1936, Mizoguchi Kenji)
Shiganoya Benkei, Yamada Isuzu

Style openly parallels story, and all this is accomplished with a comic awareness which the West would not see in such polished form until the films of Jacques Tati.

At the same time that *gendaigeki* directors were creating or assimilating such new styles, they were also concerning themselves with new themes, most importantly with a social criticism of Japan analogous to the outspoken censure in the earlier *jidaigeki*. Ozu's *I Was Born, But ...* exposes various inequalities and criticizes a society in which they are allowed to exist. Ozu was as critical as Ito had been in his *jidaigeki*. Both said that something ought to be done about Japanese society, one using humour and the other violence.

Film as a tool of social criticism was something new. In such pictures as *Souls on the Road* and *The Kyoya Collar Shop* it was not society but 'fate' which brought about the tragedies. The appropriate response was: it cannot be helped, we must put up with it. During the early 1930s, however, an oppressive government and a too docile society were openly held responsible for tragic events.

There were various reasons for such uncommon candour: an economic depression in Japan, the egalitarian example of the United States, and the populist promise of Marxism. Through the new realism the indifference of the government and the coldness of society could be criticized.

The young Uchida Tomu made *A Live Doll* (Ikeru ningyo, 1929) about the unthinking cruelty of a calloused society; the protean Mizoguchi in one year, 1929, made *Tokyo March* (Tokyo koshinkyoku) and *Metropolitan Symphony* (Tokai kokyogaku), both of which contrasted the life of the proletariat with that of the well-to-do. The big hit of 1930, and the largest moneymaker in the history of Japanese film till then, was *What Made Her Do It?* (Naniga kanojo o so saseta ka), directed by Suzuki Shigeyoshi, a particularly outspoken picture about a poor girl and her fate in a cruel and uncaring society.

These films, which grew ever more critical of an authoritarian society, formed that short-lived genre, the *keiko-eiga*, a term sometimes loosely translated as 'tendency film', itself a euphemism for movies with definite political overtones. Just how leftist these pro-proletariat pictures were, however, is a matter still being discussed. At least one of the directors, Furumi Takuji, went to Russia and came back a communist. At the same time these message films of the period are filled with an almost American concern for 'the little man'.

The tendency films which went furthest were the *jidai-geki*, a fact of which the government was well aware. As early as 1928 Makino's *Street of Masterless Samurai* had been heavily cut before its release. Another film which did not escape the censor's scissors was Ito's *Man-Slashing, Horse-Piercing Sword*, which denounces the 'exploiting classes', all quite recognizable under their samurai armour.

Uchida's *Revenge Champion* (Adauchi senshu, 1931) and Itami's *Peerless Patriot* (Kokushi muso, 1932) even dispense with sword-play altogether in the interests of social comment. The latter film, through a plot involving swordsman samurai and a *ronin* imposter, shows the latter beating the lord at his own game, and thus manages to question hereditary rule.

Itami's *Akanishi Kakita* (1936) goes farthest in the humanization of the samurai. The hero cares more for his pet cat than for his girlfriend, he is not impressed with his superiors, and he suffers from stomach-aches. With samurai Kakita the way is clear for those later, post-war samurai and *ronin* heroes who so resemble him. In fact, 'when [Kurosawa's] Yojimbo first appears on the screen, swinging his shoulders in his characteristic manner, he is walking straight out of the tradition of Susukita Rokuhei.'[25]

Perhaps the finest of these humanistic, socially critical *jidaigeki* were made by a group of Kyoto scenarists and directors including Yamanaka Sadao, a director who in a short career made several of the most memorable period films. One was *Kochiyama Soshun* (1936), a deliberate parody of a Kawatake Mokuami Kabuki drama in which feudal precepts are satirized and highminded ideals are humanized. The gambler Kochiyama, a true common man, fights against repressive authority and dies for what he believes in.

Many, however, consider Yamanaka's best film to be *Humanity and Paper Balloons* (Ninjo kami fusen, 1937), a realistically detailed picture of *ronin* life rendered moving by the conscious confines of its presentation. A masterless samurai has sold his sword to buy rice, and his wife makes children's balloons in order to bring in a little money. They live in a poor tenement, and eventually die through innocent involvement in a petty crime. Social criticism is present in every scene and each is made memorable by the employment of a realism of the most selective and telling kind.

There are two areas of acting space: the tenement and the town. The former is so rigorously reticulated that the viewer soon comes to know it intimately; the latter, the town, which so threatens those in the tenement, is on the contrary, not charted at all. The viewer becomes no less confused than the characters as soon as they venture out. Shots inside the tenement are usually right angled and the acting is frontal, both conventions which the Japanese associate with stability. Outside, the camera position seems by contrast arbitrary.[26] In any event, the camera is usually stationary. The kind of freedom associated with

*A Star Athlete* (Hanagata senshu, 1937, Shimizu Hiroshi)
Sano Shuji

*Humanity and Paper Balloons* (Ninjo kami fusen, 1937, Yamanaka Sadao)
Nakamura Kanemon, Kawarazaki Chojuro, Suketakaya Sukezo

the moving camera is one which the nature of Yamanaka's story seeks to deny.

These and other polarities in the film create a reality stripped down, reduced and hence extremely powerful.[27] The humanist morality of the film is illuminated by the logical formality of its construction. Social criticism is apparent in its very form.

Though the authorities may have been blind to the film's artistry they were certainly aware of its import. By 1937 the government had gained all but complete control of the film industry, militarists had assumed power, and any promise of democratic freedom had vanished. An authoritarian government had turned totalitarian, a staged invasion of China would soon result in war, and Tokugawa-style repression had returned. In motion pictures all *keiko* films were banned, the proscription soon extended to all films which questioned loyalty as well as to all critical and realistic *jidaigeki*. Shortly after Yamanaka had made *Humanity and Paper Balloons* he was sent to the China front where he died.

# 3
# The 1940s and the 1950s

As the military took over the civilian government, much that was liberal and anti-authoritarian in Japanese life was suppressed. Formal appeals were issued to 'imbue the minds of the young with a military spirit' and opposition was made ineffectual.

Films, considered part of the public media, were the first to suffer. Even in the early 1930s the official censors had begun cutting foreign films: the pacific *All Quiet on the Western Front* suffered nearly three hundred cuts before being shown in Japan. Now the military censors were strong enough to dictate local film policy as well.

The concept of government-controlled 'national policy films' (*senikoyo-eiga*) appeared as early as 1932, its purpose being to aid and perhaps excuse Japan's military adventures. As the army gained greater control, more ideological films were required. In 1936 the industry was placed under the Ministry of Home Affairs and the Media Section of the Imperial Army. From 1939 the all-encompassing Motion Picture Law ordered the exclusive production of national policy films.

Initially these films stressed 'the human face of war', and attendant horrors were minimized. In pictures such as Tasaka Tomotaka's *Five Scouts* (Gonin no sekkohei, 1938) and *Mud and Soldiers* (Tsuchi to heitai, 1939) the open, friendly soldiers give their all for emperor and country, but no footage is devoted to portraying the enemy. The Japanese audience did not require such dramatization because the duty of going to war was unquestioned and it was not necessary to portray the bestiality of the enemy.

After the attack on Pearl Harbour in December 1941 which marked the beginning of the Pacific War, the tone of the national policy films changed. There was greater emphasis upon the attractive camaraderie of military life, and the spiritual benefits of such an education. Taguchi Tetsu's *Generals, Staff and Soldiers* (Shogun to sambo to hei, 1942), starring the former *ronin* hero, Bando Tsumasaburo, and Yamamoto Kajiro's *The War at Sea from Hawaii to Malaya* (Hawai-Marei oki kaisen, 1942) highlights such benefits, while completely neglecting the extreme brutality with which recruits were increasingly treated.

At the same time the people back home were shown that they too had their duties. Naruse's *The Whole Family Works* (Hataraku ikka, 1939) carries just that message, and Kurosawa's *The Most Beautiful* (Ichiban utsukushiku, 1944) shows the whole factory working.

It was only later that the kind of anti-enemy propaganda the West associates with wartime cinema was insisted upon. In 1940 Yoshimura Kimisaburo could make a film about the noble humanity of a staff officer in *The Story of Tank Commander Nishizumi* (Nishizumi senshacho-den); by 1943 he was forced to make *The Spy Isn't Yet Dead* (Kancho imada shisezu), about the machinations of enemy agents in Japan and the horrible American who controls them.

One result of all this governmental control was that stylistic influences from the West were considerably lessened; there had indeed been criticism that foreign ways were taking over the native product. When the new Western-style PCL Studio was built it was playfully averred that the initials stood not for Photo Chemical Laboratory but for Pork Cutlet Lard, something which the lean fish-eating Japanese associated with the gross West.[28]

*Empire of the Senses* (Ai no koriida, 1976, Oshima Nagisa)
Matsuda Eiko

*Third Base* (Saado, 1978, Higashi Yoichi)
Nagashima Toshiyuki

*Far Thunder* (Enrai, 1981, Negishi Yoshitaro)
Ishida Eri, Nagashima Toshiyuki

*The Family Game* (Kazoku geimu, 1984, Morita Yoshimitsu)
Yuki Saori, Itami Juzo, Matsuda Yusaku, Miyagawa Ichirota, Tsujita Junichi

More seriously, there were official objections to noticeably 'foreign styles'. The Army's Media Section strongly criticized both the style and content of Kurosawa's début film, *Sanshiro Sugata* (Sugata Sanshiro, 1943), and the film might not have been released if Ozu Yasujiro, sitting on the board as a representative of the studio, had not won the authorities over.

There was, consequently, a conscious move back to whatever Japan still retained of a 'national' style. This resulted in a number of historical pageants such as Uchida's *History* (Rekishi, 1940), originally a three-part epic though only the first was completed, and Kinugasa's *The Battle of Kawanakajima* (Kawanakajima kassen, 1941). However, the 'national' style was by now so completely an amalgam of international influences that any attempt to regain a purely 'Japanese' vision or to proscribe stylistic imports could not be successful. None the less there was in Japan's wartime cinema not much fast cutting and very little camera movement for its own sake. Mizoguchi's *The Genroku Loyal Forty-seven Ronin* (1941), a two-part version of a new (1937) Kabuki rewriting of *Chushingura*, is notable for its stately tempos and its stage-like settings. This series of tableaux does indeed resemble the Japanese film of thirty years before except that its apparent simplicities are those of sophistication, knowledge and intent.

Another example of a return to native ways was Uchida's *Earth* (Tsuchi, 1939). Based on the 1910 novel by Nagatsuka Takashi, it portrays what Natsume Soseki in his preface to the book had called the plight of the 'wretched farmers, without education or refinement'.

Uchida matched the candid simplicity of the book with a near-documentary style. He offered no solutions to agrarian ills. Those looking for a return to native values could find it in this chronicle of the seasons, a demonstra-

*Earth* (Tsuchi, 1939, Uchida Tomu)
Kazami Akiko, Kosugi Isamu

*Ikiru* (1952, Kurosawa Akira)
Odagiri Miki, Shimura Takashi

tion of the links between man and nature, and the highly selective detail which connected the slight story strands. Actually, the film was made without official permission, but its success prompted the authorities to claim that it showed Japanese farmers patriotically putting up with their lot.

Most of the national policy films were devoid of both honesty and interest, and as the war continued film production, for a number of reasons, steadily declined. During the 1930s Japan had produced some five hundred features each year, making it second in production only to the United States. By 1941 the number had halved and in 1945, the year in which the war ended with the defeat of Japan, only 26 films were made.

The rehabilitation of the film industry was among the goals of the Allied Occupation Forces. The Motion Picture Law was rescinded and, in its place, the American Occupation Army's Civil Information and Education Section began defining what was permissible.

These rules were just as detailed as those of the censorship offices which they had supplanted. The Americans issued a list of 13 forbidden subjects, the most serious being 'feudal loyalty', the very subject that had constituted the major theme of Japanese wartime cinema. In the spring of 1946 the United States Eighth Army lit a large bonfire to burn those films not to be kept for 'further analysis' or sent to the Library of Congress.

Some films suffered doubly in this ideological reversal. Kurosawa's *They Who Tread on the Tiger's Tail* (Tora no o o fumu otokotachi, 1945) had been criticized by the Japanese authorities for its irreverent treatment of a Kabuki classic and denied distribution. Now the American authorities banned it outright because it portrayed 'feudal loyalty', which in turn made it 'anti-democratic'. The film was not released until 1954, after the Occupation was safely over.

The continued 'feudal threat' of this battered and beaten nation was keenly felt by the Civil Information and Education Section. At one point Japanese script writers were even instructed not to include the ordinary Japanese custom of bowing: it was felt to be anti-democratic. In this and other ways Japanese writers and directors found that they could not show their own people as they actually were but only as they would be were they successfully 'democratized'.

Details of the American code were listed in a series of bulletins aimed at making a new kind of 'national policy film', one diametrically opposed to the wartime product but just as unrealistic. The idea behind the bulletins seemed to be the making of Japan into an ideal America, and to this end directors responded as best they could.

Mizoguchi Kenji presented an intended film about the printmaker Utamaro as a celebration of a pre-Occupation democrat, one beloved by the common people. He received permission but the finished film — *Utamaro and Five Women* (Utamaro o meguru gonin no onna, 1946) — much dismayed the original author, Kunieda Kanji, who had emphasized the much more daring theme of freedom through eroticism.

Permission was also granted for the making of a whole series of new Kunisada Chuji films by various hands. One might have thought that the Civil Information and Education Section, having banned *Chushingura* and most other period fare, would have frowned upon so notorious a *jidaigeki* hero. However, they allowed it to go ahead, having been persuaded that this low-class gambler *yakuza* was really a democratic fighter for justice, a hero of the people.

What the Occupation authorities really wanted were 'American-style' *gendaigeki*: fast, modern and optimistic. Kissing, for example, was a democratic custom hitherto absent from the Japanese cinema. The taboo was consequently broken in two new films which premièred on the same day in the spring of 1946.

More seriously, the Civil Information and Education Section encouraged pictures which criticized the old order and indicated hope for a new society. This policy resulted in a number of interesting films, among them Kurosawa's *No Regrets for Our Youth* (Waga seishun ni kui nashi, 1946), Kinoshita Keisuke's *A Morning with the Osone Family* (Osone-ke no asa, 1946) and Yoshimura's *A Ball at the Anjo House* (Anjo-ke no butokai, 1947) — all of them about the consequences of Japan's wartime policies and how individuals now had the freedom to make their own choices.

There were many such attempts at individuality, something wanted by both the Occupation authorities and the Japanese. The wartime years had seen a return to totalitarian times; now individuality could be openly celebrated.

This is not to imply that individuality did not exist during the war years. There were directors such as Ozu Yasujiro who in 1942 created one of his most individual and personal films, *There Was a Father* (Chichi ariki), one in which the war effort played no role, and one in which the individuality of both father and son (to say nothing of the individuality of Ozu) was wonderfully affirmed.

Now, however, individuality was officially approved. This meant that writers and directors were free to express, discover, or create personal styles. They were now also free to study and draw upon a wide range of Western cinematic styles and techniques. Earlier the critic Iwasaki Akira had complained that 'the close-up, flash-back, dissolve, all such foreign techniques were dragged in un-digested, then indiscriminately used'.[29] This was no longer true. Things borrowed become truly one's own. In the post-war years foreign techniques were thoroughly adapted for the purposes that foreign directors had intended them to serve.

At the same time other aspects of the industry were manifesting foreign influences, mainly American, resulting in stronger unions and major strikes. The industry had been traditionally hierarchic, with directors coming up through the ranks. An aspirant would attach himself to the unit of a major director and in due course become first assistant. Some did not make their own films until well into middle age. Now, however, the new post-war freedom was affecting even studio administration.

Kurosawa, Kinoshita, Ichikawa, Imai Tadashi and Shindo Kaneto were among the directors who rose rapidly during the post-war years. The old system could no longer hold them back and the new system encouraged them.

The studios, financially secure with their enormous post-war audiences, gave directors a great deal of freedom. For the first time studios supported novel projects. The result was a directorial freedom the Japanese cinema had never known and this in turn led to a proliferation of new genres and new films.

Japanese film had long been considered generic as the absolute polarity of *jidaigeki* and *gendaigeki* and all of the sub-genres in between suggests. There were, in addition, many other genres, among them the famous *haha-mono*, films about mother. After the war genres both increased and metamorphosed. The *haha-mono*, for example, became the *tsuma-mono* (films about wives), indicating the new importance of the marriage partner in post-war Japan, and also the growing new segment of the cinema audience.

In addition to revivals of genres there was the creation of many new ones. Japan took early to the monster picture (though not the horror film) and, given the nation's predisposition to the presentational, it is not surprising that it early adapted the animated film and continues to excel in the genre. There was also, more importantly, a new kind of comedy-satire.

In pre-war Japanese cinema there had been comedy enough but, for obvious reasons, little satire. Now, however, the climate was right for some mocking of the old regime and its ways. Kinoshita deflated the authoritarian father in *The Broken Drum* (Yabure daiko, 1949), with ex-*ronin* Bando Tsumasaburo as the newly impotent parent; in *Carmen's Pure Love* (Karumen junjosu, 1952) he poked fun at the remnants of feudalism in the new democratized Japan. The younger Ichikawa Kon satirized both pre-war values and post-war pretensions in *Mr Pu* (Pu-san, 1953), *A Billionaire* (Okuman choja, 1954) and *A Crowded Streetcar* (Manin densha, 1957).

These new subjects and new directors reflected new aspirations. Personifying them were the stars. Tanaka Kinuyo, Yamada Isuzu and Hara Setsuko were actresses who had weathered the war years and now harboured hopes for the coming age; newcomers included Takamine Hideko, Mifune Toshiro, Kyo Machiko and Mori Masayuki.

Directors, both old and new, began making films which depicted Japanese life not as it should have been but as they saw it. This meant that a realistic mode became for the first time necessary to Japanese cinema. The problem facing the director was how to combine the demands of a further realism with the constraints of the Japanese aesthetic.

The films of Kurosawa reflected these concerns. For example, they look quite real but are mostly studio shot.

*One Wonderful Sunday* (Subarashiki nichiyobi, 1947), *Drunken Angel* (Yoidore tenshi, 1948) and *Stray Dog* (Nora inu, 1948) appear to be *neorealismo*, and have been so called, but their realism is consciously designed, with details far more meticulously selected than is common in similar films in the West. Likewise, when Imai Tadashi revived the *keiko* film and portrayed the poor by putting actors on the streets in *And Yet We Live* (Dokkoi ikiteiru, 1951), when Shindo shot *Children of the Atom Bomb* (Gembaku no ko, 1952) in Hiroshima itself, when Shimizu Hiroshi used genuine street urchins in *Children of the Beehive* (Hachi no su no kodomotachi, 1948), the resulting realism in all these films was not that of a De Sica or a Rossellini because the assumptions of the directors were different.

Raw reality could have small part in the Japanese cinema when there was such chaos in Japan itself, but a selective realism could. And, at the same time, the new styles and techniques could be rendered acceptable, that is, Japanese.

The post-war Kurosawa films, for example, are not structured like the foreign films which they may superficially resemble. *Drunken Angel* has no plot, just parallel stories; *Stray Dog* is a theme with variations, the theme being the anecdote (cop loses gun) on which the entire film is hung; *One Wonderful Sunday*, based on an early Griffith film, is structurally naïve, and purposely so. It is much more like an American film of 1920 than of 1950.

After finishing *One Wonderful Sunday* Kurosawa was asked about foreign influences, particularly those in editing. He replied: 'Whenever we get down to talking about editing, the issue of montage is immediately brought up. I cannot but feel, however, that these theories are strange aberrations of the imagination. When it comes to the basics of film technique I am a naïve Griffithean.'[30] And

46

*Ugetsu* (Ugetsu monogatari, 1953, Mizoguchi Kenji)
Kyo Machiko, Mori Masayuki

*Tokyo Story* (Tokyo monogatari, 1953, Ozu Yasujiro)
Hara Setsuko, Ryu Chishu

the Griffith style was one which had enough common ground with early Japanese perceptions of film to be perennially acceptable.

When Sergei Eisenstein said in 1929 that 'the principle of montage can be identified as the basic element of Japanese representational culture', he could not have been thinking of Japanese film. The Russian found justification for his theories in the *kanji* characters of the Japanese language and in the *haiku* of Japanese poetry, but Japanese film is of the same lineage as drama rather than poetry, and the premises are not the same.

The literary influence is there but it shows itself in a different and more oblique fashion. It affects cinematic expression, not cinematic means. The Japanese literary style has been described as supporting or creating a narrative which 'depends much more on what might be termed lyric insight than on the clash of personality and political power'. It moves 'inward with a narrative line pushing beyond story, often beyond character, to a general realm of feeling'.[31]

This is as true of the Japanese film as it is of the Japanese novel, and in both there is the creation of a kind of atmosphere which becomes a true 'realm of feeling'. This results in a detailed and real-appearing world which defines an often unarticulated series of stories and a group of otherwise amorphous characters.

The example is, again, Mizoguchi Kenji. After the war he continued to make a series of historical films which examined the past as though it were the present and showed a concern for that realistic detail which could reveal fundamental values and lyrical insight. The result was a strongly aesthetic style.

*The Life of Oharu* (Saikaku ichidai onna, 1952) was based on the Saikaku novel, but where the original was a realistic and picaresque account of the downfall of a willing courtesan, Yoda and Mizoguchi created a lyric elegy, more parable than cautionary tale. The famous *Ugetsu* (Ugetsu monogatari, 1953), based on two ghost stories of Ueda Akinari, were simplified into a moving allegory of love, sacred and profane. *Sansho the Bailiff* (Sansho dayu, 1954), based on a Mori Ogai story in turn derived from a medieval account, and *A Story from Chikamatsu* (aka *The Crucified Lovers*, Chikamatsu monogatari, 1954) based on a well-known Bunraku play, created a world in which realistic details revealed emotional nuances, and the injustices of feudal life were regarded with a detached and contemplative eye.

In these last films made two years before his death in 1956 Mizoguchi displayed the culmination of his style. These pictures indeed appear to 'unroll like a seamless scroll . . . in which tableaux [are] photographed from an imperial distance and then cut together . . . two moments of balance, beginning with the movements of the character, then coming to rest at its own proper point'.[32] References to Japanese pictorial forms are appropriate here: in Mizoguchi the traditional Japanese style is seen at its most assured.

Ozu Yasujiro continued to make the *gendaigeki* which were so completely his own. He further refined his style (no more pans after the war) while enlarging his references. With his writer, Noda Kogo, he no longer saw society as the sole cause of human predicaments. Japanese cinema had lost a social critic but gained a philosopher, for in Ozu's cosmic vision the cause of life's difficulties was life itself.

In *Late Spring* (Banshun, 1949) the story — daughter leaves widowed father to marry — questions whether contentment is possible and at the same time shows an acceptance of things as they are as the only solution, however partial. In *Tokyo Story* (Tokyo monogatari, 1953), after the death of the mother, the younger daughter asks: 'But, isn't life disappointing?', to which the daughter-in-law, with a smile of acceptance, replies: 'Yes, it is.'

This acceptance is accomplished with a directness, a laconic simplicity which is in itself the result of Ozu's radical style. The focus of the mature Ozu view, the perfect balance of the events portrayed, the subtle parallels between scenes, the irony of sudden reversals — this grid of narrative strategies creates the profound humanity of the Ozu film.

In Ozu's later films we find the ultimate criticism, a criticism of life. And this pragmatic criticism, one which has long been a part of Japanese culture itself, is affirmative. Through *Floating Weeds* (Ukigusa, 1959), *Late Autumn* (Akibiyori, 1960), to his last film, *An Autumn Afternoon* (Samma no aji, 1962), Ozu, who died in 1963, developed 'one of the most distinctive visual styles in the cinema'. Commonly attributed to 'the influence of ... traditions of Japanese art ... and a deliberate imitation of and action against Western cinema ... his style reveals vast possibilities within a narrow compass'.[33]

Another director concerned with affirmation was Gosho Heinosuke. Particularly active in the 1950s (he died in 1981), Gosho kept alive the humanistic traditions of the *shomingeki* and the concerns of his teacher and mentor, Shimazu Yasujiro. His *An Inn in Osaka* (Osaka no yado, 1954) is about people sinking into poverty but still trying to help one another; *Growing Up* (Takekurabe, 1956), based on the Higuchi Ichiyo novel, is about an innocent young girl marked for a life of prostitution in the Yoshiwara and the helplessness of those about her. The sorrows of these people are shown through close-ups and fast

*An Inn at Osaka* (Osaka no yado, 1954, Gosho Heinosuke)
Sano Shuji, Otowa Nobuko

*Seven Samurai* (Shichinin no samurai, 1954, Kurosawa Akira)
Inaba Yoshio, Mifune Toshiro, Kato Daisuke, Chiaki Minoru,
Kimura Ko, Shimura Takashi, Miyagawa Seiji

editing, a style based on Western models, particularly that of Ernst Lubitsch whose films Gosho carefully studied. It was a style which proved capable of capturing much of the flavour of the Japanese ethos. This Gosho himself called 'the bittersweet flavour of life', that mixture of tears and smiles which the Japanese audience found so appealing.

Naruse Mikio pursued his own kind of realism, one based upon close observation and selective detail. His *Repast* (Meshi, 1951), based on the last (unfinished) novel by Hayashi Fumiko, scripted by his favourite writers, Ide Toshiro and Tanaka Sumie, is about a post-war couple who, despite differences, decide to stay together. *Late Chrysanthemums* (Bangiku, 1954), another Hayashi adaptation, like the later *Flowing* (Nagareru, 1956), is about the dissolution of the old order: in both we witness the disappearance of the traditions of the old-style geisha. In the later *When a Woman Ascends the Stairs* (Onna ga kaidan o agaru toki, 1960), based on a script by Kikushima Ryuzo, we see the woman returning to her hopeless job, as many a Naruse heroine has returned to her hopeless husband, disillusioned but still retaining her own integrity.

Naruse himself (he died in 1969) said that the essential thing was 'knowing how to capture the humanity of the human condition, knowing how to portray humanness'.[34] How he does this is explained by Sato Tadao. 'He often photographs his characters in profile ... his camera has the eye of an outsider who happens to be in the right place.... As a result Naruse's camera is sometimes marvellously intimate with his characters [but] sometimes exceedingly cold.' This Sato finds unlike Ozu who 'assumes the attitude of meeting an acquaintance. [His] films do not investigate'.[35]

It is Naruse's analytical intimacy that informs his finest films. In *Floating Clouds* (Ukigumo, 1955), yet another

Hayashi story, scripted by Mizuki Yoko, the camera stares at the actors in the final scene with a gaze which refuses comment as the man, only now realizing the worth of the woman, helps prepare her corpse. It is a moment of gravity, of utter stillness, rare in cinema. It is pure presentation.

It is this quality (presentation, of a very different manner) which Ozu had in mind when he reportedly told Naruse that the two films which he himself could never have made, much as he might have wanted to, were Mizoguchi's *Sisters of the Gion* and Naruse's own *Floating Clouds*.[36]

Among the directors who had begun their careers during the Pacific War it was Kurosawa Akira who, more than anyone, helped to perpetuate one of the major genres of the Japanese cinema with a series of *jidaigeki* which were inspired by those films of Ito, Itami and Yamanaka made in the late 1930s. They were filled with a convincing if highly selective realism, owed nothing at all to the operatics of the *chambara* (a minor genre which even in post-war Japan kept the ingredients of the old Matsunosuke spectacular), and continued the sober humanism of the finest period films.

Though *Rashomon* (1950) is not really a *jidaigeki* — it is set in the twelfth century while *jidaigeki* are commonly thought to belong to the Tokugawa period (1603–1867) — it is filled with a rigour, a seriousness and a healthy scepticism typical of the best period films of the 1930s. Written by Kurosawa and Hashimoto Shinobu after several stories by Akutagawa Ryunosuke, this investigation of a rape and murder told through flashbacks questions not only 'truth' but also 'reality' in a manner as 'nihilistic' as any pre-war period director could have wished, and then, in the post-war manner, affirms them none the less.

*Seven Samurai* (Shichinin no samurai, 1954), written by Kurosawa, Hashimoto and Oguni Hideo, with its story of a band of *ronin* coming to the rescue of a group of bandit-beleaguered farmers, could have been written by Itami or Yamanaka, so close are its liberal aims to theirs. Kurosawa's later *jidaigeki* comedies, *Yojimbo* (1961) and *Sanjuro* (Tsubaki Sanjuro, 1962), both scripted with Kikushima Ryuzo, and that affectionate satire of the common *chambara, The Hidden Fortress* (Kakushi toride no san-akunin, 1958), written by Kurosawa's best scenarists (Hashimoto, Oguni, Kikushima and himself), are funny in the same way that Itami's *Kakita Akanishi* and Yamanaka's *Sazen Tange: The Million Ryo Pot* (Tange Sazen — Hyakuman ryo no tsubo, 1935) and *Kochiyama Soshun* are: pretensions are exposed and malice overcome through the simple humanity of the samurai hero.

At the same time, Kurosawa's *jidaigeki* are influenced by foreign styles. They owe much to American films, especially to Westerns, in particular, says the director, to those of John Ford. What he has assimilated from the West is also seen clearly in his *gendaigeki*, particularly in the finest of them all, *Ikiru* (1952).

A man dying of cancer seeks to affirm himself, and manages to do so. The script, by Hashimoto, Oguni and Kurosawa, combines an authoritative voice and a deliberately revealing structure with a highly selective naturalism to create a style which blends social realism with lyricism in a way that is deeply moving and very Japanese. This film also marked the beginning of an interest in expressionism (the celebrated 'night-town' sequence) which grew through such films as *The Idiot* (Hakuchi, 1951) and *Dodesukaden* (1970) to the mannered cinema of *Kagemusha* (1980) and *Ran* (1985).

Another post-war continuation of pre-war interests was

*Fire Festival* (Hi matsuri, 1985, Yanagimachi Mitsuo)
Kitaoji Kinya

*The Funeral* (Ososhiki, 1985, Itami Juzo)
Miyamoto Nobuko, Bito Isao, Sugai Kin

*Typhoon Club* (Taifu kurabu, 1986, Somai Shinji)
Mikami Yuichi, Kudo Yuki

the steady stream of literary adaptations. While it is true that the cinema in most countries draws heavily from plays, novels and stories for its plots, the Japanese film does this to a greater extent and seems to suffer a greater lack of original film scenarios.

Japanese adaptations, unlike those of the West, seldom encompass the work in its entirety. For example, of the several versions of *The Tale of Genji* (Yoshimura's in 1952, Ichikawa's for television in the 1960s, and an animated cartoon version in 1985), none is complete. The Japanese way of adapting was defined by Naruse: 'I'm no good at directing long stories and novels. My films based on short stories or excerpts from novels have always been much more successful. I'm good at expanding but no good at compressing.'[37]

In this Naruse resembles most Japanese directors. Mizoguchi enlarged upon the kernel of the stories he chose; Ozu expanded the anecdote, or sometimes no more than a line or two of dialogue that he and Noda had chosen. Though there have been long, usually routine, re-enactments of lengthy plays and novels, such as the various films based on *Chushingura* and on the popular historical novel, *Miyamoto Musashi*, the majority of adaptations have been faithless to the form of the original but, if well conceived, true to the spirit.

Imai Tadashi adapted three stories by Higuchi Ichiyo and merged them in *Troubled Waters* (aka *Muddy Waters*, Nigorie, 1953), a film about women and their problems in the Meiji era. In 1958 he made his finest film, *Night Drum* (Yoru no tsuzumi), scripted by Hashimoto after a Chikamatsu doll-drama. The central episode of the play, in which a wife has an affair during her husband's absence, is condensed, while the dénouement, in which the husband kills the adulterous couple as custom decrees and is then faced with a life which he himself has rendered meaning-less, is emphasized.

Another socially committed director, Kobayashi Masaki, made one of the most financially successful post-war adaptations in the three-part *Human Condition* (Ningen no joken, 1958–61). These long films were based upon the even longer best-selling Gomikawa Junpei novel about an idealistic Japanese soldier unhappy at Japan's brutal ex-ploitation of Manchuria. Kobayashi's *Harakiri* (Seppuku, 1962), after an original script by Hashimoto Shinobu, is one of the strongest indictments of the samurai ethos, and is in the same lineage as the dissident *jidaigeki* of the 1920s and 30s. However, Kobayashi remains best known for his most spectacular adaptation, that of a number of short Lafcadio Hearn ghost stories in *Kwaidan* (Kaidan, 1965), and for the questioning, fragmented documentary, com-piled from post-war newsreels, *The Tokyo Trial* (Tokyo saiban, 1983).

Kobayashi had served as assistant director to Kinoshita Keisuke who, after his early successes with the new com-edy satire, turned to somewhat orthodox adaptations. One of the most popular was the sentiment-filled *Twenty-Four Eyes* (Nijushi no hitomi, 1954), the story of Japan from 1927 to 1946 seen through the eyes of an elementary-school teacher. It was based on the popular novel by Tsuboi Sakae, and his next film was based on a popular Ito Sachio novel. *She Was Like a Wild Chrysanthemum* (Nogiku no gotoki kimi nariki, 1955) is about an old man returning to the scenes of his youth and remembering his lost love, a theme rendered even more nostalgic by the film's visual approximation to late nineteenth-century photographs.

Kinoshita's most famous adaptation is probably *The Ballad of Narayama* (Narayama bushiko, 1958), based on the short Fukazawa Shichiro novel about the apocryphal

*Twenty-four Eyes* (Nijushi no hitomi, 1954, Kinoshita Keisuke)
Takamine Hideko

*Marital Relations* (Meoto zenzai, 1955, Toyoda Shiro)
Awashima Chikage, Morishige Hisaya

custom of leaving the aged to die on a mountain top, a story to be filmed again in 1983 by Imamura Shohei. In it Kinoshita deliberately uses the conventions of the Kabuki to remove from this folktale any realist pretensions. In *The River Fuefuki* (Fuefukigawa, 1960), another adaptation of a work by Fukazawa, a saga of three generations of a family during the civil wars of the sixteenth century, Kinoshita seeks to recount his period story in a period manner: partial colouring of scenes in the manner of early *ukiyo-e* prints, long scroll-like dollies and asymmetrical compositions — a self-conscious reconstruction of a Japanese style.

Some of the finest of these adaptations, ones particularly distinguished by that atmospheric realism so characteristic of post-war Japanese films, were directed by Toyoda Shiro. He very successfully adapted Oda Sakunosuke's *Marital Relations* (Meoto zenzai, 1955), a wry comedy about a geisha and her no-good lover, creating a modern version of the *michiyuki*, the lovers' flight, that standard feature of the Osaka doll-drama. Equally expert was his adaptation of Tanizaki's *A Cat, Shozo and Two Women* (Neko to Shozo to futari no onna, 1956), a comedy made, as the title indicates, out of very little. Toyoda's film version was created through equally few means — a set or two, the seashore — and well captured the appropriate lightness. In *A Tale from East of the River* (aka *Twilight Story*, Bokuto kidan, 1960) one of Nagai Kafu's most evocative stories, set in the old prostitute quarter of Tamanoi, was recreated on the studio lot, with the surroundings appearing to be an extension of the actors, an environment designed, as in the earliest films, to comment upon the feelings of the characters.

Another successful adapter was Ichikawa Kon who, like Kinoshita, turned from satire to more standard fare.

Among the first and most successful of his adaptations was *Kokoro* (1955), a very free version of the Natsume Soseki classic. More popular was *The Harp of Burma* (Biruma no tategoto, 1956), based on the Takeyama Michio novel and also scripted by the late Wada Natto, Ichikawa's wife.

It was she who had worked with the director since 1949 and scripted all of his later successful films. Among these were *Conflagration* (Enjo, 1958), a version of Mishima Yukio's *The Temple of the Gold Pavilion; Fires on the Plain* (Nobi, 1958) after the Ooka Shohei wartime story; *The Key* (aka *Odd Obsession*, Kagi, 1959) from the Tanizaki novel; *Bonchi* (1961) based on the Yamazaki Toyoko novel; *Younger Brother* (aka *Her Brother*, Ototo, 1961) after the Koda Aya novel; and *The Outcast* (aka *The Broken Commandment*, Hakai, 1962) based on the Shimazaki Toson novel.

In all of these much of the success was due to the economy with which Wada used the originals. None are seen in their complete form and some, like *The Key*, are completely altered. An indication of Wada's success may be seen in her radical adaptation of Soseki's *Kokoro* which leaves out much of the original yet retains its quintessential atmosphere. The failure of a later Soseki adaptation, Ichikawa's *I Am a Cat* (Wagahai wa neko de aru, 1975), may be accounted for by another script-writer's attempt to include too much of the original story.

The finest of these films provided Ichikawa with the opportunity to display his ravishing visual style, one so bold that it has been called graphic: the asymmetric arrangement of black against white in *The Outcast*; the complicated balance of the long family-conference scene in *The Key*; the purely pictorial rendering of water in the swimming scenes in *Kokoro*; the scroll-like setting of men against scene in *The Wanderers* (Matatabi, 1973), scripted by Tanikawa Shuntaro. Herein lies another reason for their success.

Perhaps the most concentrated example of this style, and the single most successful Ichikawa–Wada collaboration, is *An Actor's Revenge* (Yukinojo henge, 1963), a deliberately faithful remake of the old Ito Daisuke–Kinugasa Teinosuke script. In it Ichikawa delights in the old-fashioned conventions of both the stage (the hero is a Kabuki female impersonator) and early Japanese film, particularly the more spectacular *jidaigeki* of Ito and Makino. The female-impersonator hero was played by the ageing pre-war matinée idol Hasegawa Kazuo, and the result is a stylish film filled with nostalgia and an affectionate irony.

At the same time that Japanese cinema was carrying on the tradition of studio-built realism there was a small but growing concern for the kind of realism known as documentary. This change began, as in the days of Osanai, with a small number of directors criticizing the film as it was, calling for something closer to 'truth'.

Not surprisingly, there had never been a true documentary tradition in Japan, a country where a rather more elaborate presentation was insisted upon. Documentary was thought too raw for Japanese taste. None the less, directors who had tired of the studio look and its limitations began in the 1950s to incorporate documentary-like techniques into their films.

Older directors such as Shimizu Hiroshi began using amateurs in real surroundings. Leftist directors such as Imai and Sekigawa Hideo reasoned that photographic realism enhanced a political realism. Even so conservative a director as Kinoshita used newsreel footage to make events 'real' in *A Japanese Tragedy* (Nihon no higeki, 1954);

*Floating Clouds* (Ukigumo, 1955, Naruse Mikio)
Takamine Hideko, Mori Masayuki

*Conflagration* (Enjo, 1958, Ichikawa Kon)
Kagawa Ryosuke, Ichikawa Raizo, Nakamura Ganjiro

*Bad Boys* (Furyo shonen, 1961, Hani Susumu)
Yamada Yukio

*Harakiri* (Seppuku, 1962, Kobayashi Masaki)
Tamba Tetsuro, Nakadai Tatsuya

and Shindo Kaneto shot the whole of *The Island* (Hadaka no shima, 1960) on location, although his use of seasoned actors in all roles mitigated the realism he had wanted to achieve.

It was not, however, until the 1960s that the 'documentary approach' and the further realism that it implied appeared in any integrated form. The first documentary-like film was Hani Susumu's *Bad Boys* (Furyo shonen, 1961), about a reformatory. A real reform school, amateurs, hidden cameras, spontaneous dialogue — all were used to create a realistic picture of the juvenile dilemma.

At the same time, Hani shaped and smoothed his realism through unobtrusive but real direction, through carefully paced scenes and precise camera placement. This was not *cinéma-vérité* but Japanese-style documentary. It was also one more step away from the theatrical conventions which still to an extent shaped the Japanese cinema. One step nearer an international realist style, it remained a new kind of *Japanese* film.

# 4
# From the 1960s to the 1980s

THERE were various reasons for the appearance of a new kind of film in Japan in the 1960s. Among them was the competition of television. In 1958 annual admissions were at a thousand million; ten years later the figure had fallen to three hundred million. Moreover, during this decade more than half of the cinemas in the country had closed. At the same time, the number of television sets in the country increased from two million in 1958 to over twenty-two million in 1969.[38]

Film companies were thus inclined to listen to young, dissatisfied directors, something they would not have done a decade earlier or, for that matter, a decade later. Complaints that Japanese films offered no real reflection of Japanese life, that Mizoguchi was *engeki-teki* (stagey) and Ozu *furukusai* (old-fashioned), were listened to with patience.

The first of these vocal new directors was Masumura Yasuzo who called for nothing less than the destruction of mainstream Japanese cinema. He argued that it advocated suppression of individual personality, that it was congruent only with Japan's literary tradition, that all of the characters in these films invariably submitted to a collective self, that even in leftist films the heroes deferred to the will of the masses.

The motion picture companies agreed. If this was what the young thought then they should be listened to since it was the young ticket-buyer whom companies wished to attract. Thus Masumura was able to make a number of films that were fairly outspoken for their time. In *Giants and Toys* (Kyojin to gangu, 1958), scripted by Shirasaka Yoshio, he attacks the institution of television itself in this story of a television executive who refuses to submit to the dictates of showbiz.

Though Masumura was, ironically, to remain with his old-fashioned and repressive company (Daiei) long after the other young dissidents had gone independent, his films did help inspire a new kind of picture.

The young Oshima Nagisa describes his reaction after seeing the sequence of the flight of the rebel couple, shot with a hand-held camera following their motor bike, in Masumura's *Kisses* (Kuchizuke, 1957). He 'felt that the tide of the new age could no longer be ignored ... that a powerful, irresistible force had arrived in the Japanese cinema.'[39]

Another liberating influence was the popular new commercial genre of *taiyozoku* (sun-tribe) films, a series about the rebellious young. Named after the novel *Season of the Sun* (Taiyo no kisetsu) by Ishihara Shintaro, it inspired not only young directors but even such established figures as Ichikawa and Kinoshita.

The best of the *taiyozoku* films, and one which Oshima said 'heralded a new age in the Japanese cinema', was Nakahira Ko's *Crazed Fruit* (aka *Affair at Kamakura*, Kurutta kajitsu, 1956). Based on an Ishihara script (and starring the novelist's young brother, Yujiro, soon to become a 'youth' star), it tells of two brothers, one rebellious and delinquent, the other sober and serious, both in love with a girl who was involved with a dubious foreigner. Amoral, disrespectful of authority, the story was filmed in a stripped-down, laconic style in which Oshima saw signs of the new trend in 'the sound of the girl's skirt being ripped, the roar of the motorboat slashing through the body of the brother'.[40]

It was something of this questioning, irreverent attitude that Oshima aimed at when he made his first film, *A Town of Love and Hope* (Ai to kibo no machi, 1959), in which young love is pitted against Japan's class system to create a picture full of what he himself called his 'dynamic belligerence'.[41]

Oshima's hitherto complaisant company (Shochiku) found the picture outrageous. The president even called it a *keiko* film. The company might have been prepared for a new and different product, but the belligerence of this film far exceeded its expectations. None the less, because the company had invested in Oshima he was allowed to try again, this time backed by an elaborate advertising campaign which announced the arrival of the Japanese 'New Wave', a term coined in imitation of the French *nouvelle vague*, itself another commercial invention designed to herald and publicize the films of Godard, Truffaut and Chabrol at the end of the 1950s.

Oshima's *Night and Fog in Japan* (Nihon no yoru to kiri, 1960) turned out to be so uncompromisingly polemical that it was withdrawn from the Shochiku cinemas in less than a week. With this, Oshima left the company and formed his own, a move which presaged the gradual growth of the independent Japanese cinema.

The young director's departure from his company (not the first such but certainly the most dramatic) was occasioned by his realizing that the freedom of expression he sought was not to be found there. Indeed, the original willingness of major companies to entertain experiments was based entirely upon commercial expectations. When these did not materialize, they became more 'repressive' than ever.

Oshima's primary concern in cinema is freedom of expression. When he first saw Kurosawa's *No Regrets for*

*Our Youth* as a 14-year-old schoolboy he felt that here was a real theme — a woman brave enough to act on her convictions. Though later in life Oshima the director would often criticize Kurosawa's films, the inspiration received in his youth remained.

*Death by Hanging* (Koshikei, 1968) questions the Japanese judicial system and its ways of silencing such minorities as resident Koreans. *Boy* (Shonen, 1969) is about a child trained to throw himself under cars so that his parents can claim compensation and whose lack of freedom is so extreme that at the end he refuses to testify against them. *The Ceremony* (Gishiki, 1971) shows repression in the Japanese family, played out over a quarter of a century and seen through marriages and funerals.

In *Empire of the Senses* (Ai no koriida, 1976) freedom of sexual expression was put to the test. Based on a well-known event of the 1930s in which a woman accidentally killed her lover and took something to remember him by, the film asked if it is forbidden to show the act of love. The answer of the Japanese authorities was resoundingly affirmative: the film was mutilated before local showings. A protracted court case ensued, and to this day the unexpurgated version of the film cannot be shown in Japan.

Oshima's style is often as radical as his subject-matter. He usually writes his own scripts (though he sometimes works with Tamura Tsutomu, Sasaki Mamoru and Ishido Toshiro, among others) and his structuring is both documentary-like and frankly theatrical. Like Imamura and Shinoda, other members of the New Wave, Oshima comes from a theatre background, in contrast to Mizoguchi, Ozu, Kurosawa and Ichikawa, all of whom were trained in the fine arts, mainly painting. Oshima's intense interest in the theatre is manifested early in his films in an often deliberately stage-like construction, often so extreme as to be reminiscent of Makino and Matsunosuke.

The influence here is not Japanese, however, as Oshima had never seen the ancient *kyuha*. It derives, rather, from the films of Jean-Luc Godard, often overtly theatrical, which Oshima had studied, and the eclecticism of which he admired. This influence is not confined to Oshima alone. To him and his contemporaries Godard was as Lubitsch was to Ozu and Gosho: an inspiration and a point of departure.

There are, however, many differences between Oshima and Godard. Sato Tadao noted some of them when he compared the two directors' various methods of using the hand-held camera. Godard in *Au bout de souffle* wished to 'purposely fragmentize ... to willfully interrupt'. Oshima, on the other hand, uses the hand-held camera to become more intimate with his characters, creating movements which 'echo their moves, thus becoming one with them'.[42]

Oshima's ideas are confrontational but his style can seem conciliatory. Though he at times fragments his narrative, as in *The Man Who Left His Will on Film* (Tokyo senso sengo hiwa, 1970), at other times his narratives are so straightforward, as in *Boy*, that the result looks an ordinary picture until the consequences of the story are examined.

Oshima's style is eclectic in a manner that is very pragmatic and quite Japanese and he moulds it to suit the demands of each film. That *Max Mon Amour* (1987) is shot as a completely conventional film is one of the points of the picture. *Night and Fog in Japan*, a slow, dense, analytical film, has only some forty shots in it, while *Violence at Noon* (Hakuchu no torima, 1966), filled with rape and murder, has some fifteen hundred and presents a narrative

*Assassination* (Ansatsu, 1964, Shinoda Masahiro)
Tamba Tetsuro

*Intentions of Murder* (Akai satsui, 1964, Imamura Shohei)
Tsuyuguchi Shigeru, Harukawa Masumi

so shattered that the audience is left with almost no 'story' at all.

Of the intellectual Oshima, Imamura Shohei has said, 'He's a real samurai, while I'm really a farmer.'[43] In using this typical antithesis between social high and low in Japan, Imamura also meant that despite his radicalism, Oshima, a Kyoto University graduate, belongs with the intellectual élite: he is interested in ideas, in history, in politics, and presumably as much at home with Noh as he is with Shingeki.

Imamura himself, as he has often stated, is nothing of the sort. He does not even belong to 'official' Japan, a country of tea ceremony, subservient women, precisely graded degrees of social hierarchy, and such approved virtues as fidelity, loyalty and devotion. Rather, he belongs to the 'other' Japan, one which he depicts in his films and which to him is the real one.

People in Imamura's films do not behave like 'Japanese' because none of the rules of order and decorum codified by the 'official' version apply. These people (known, not suprisingly, as the 'lower classes') have not the slightest conception of fidelity or loyalty; they are a completely natural people and are to that extent uncivilized, if civilization means (as it does) a stifling of the natural.

'Many other Japanese [besides Imamura] have seen this, the primitive in the blue serge suit, but they have, almost to a man, deplored it. Very few Japanese directors have viewed and approved, though certainly Kawashima Yuzo and Ozu are among them. Most have succumbed to the idea that the Japanese must become Western as well. Imamura, however, finds this refusal, this stubborness, admirable precisely because it is this primitive naturalness that is responsible for the wholeness which the Japanese . . . still exhibit.'[44]

This 'other' Japan has as a rule been safely defused or rendered picturesque in the cinema. Even the *shomingeki* of the 1930s to this extent idealized reality — their characters usually give up. After the Second War World, however, intrusions of the 'other' Japan became more frequent, for example, in the films of Suzuki Seijun, whose farces are firmly rooted in the popular comic literature of the Tokugawa period. His is an eruption of counter-culture and, though ostensibly *gendaigeki*, might better be called Edo pop. Films such as *Tokyo Drifter* (Tokyo nagaremono, 1966) and *Elegy to Violence* (Kenka ereji, 1966) display in modern form a vital and very Japanese vulgarity.

Imamura had served as assistant director on Kawashima Yuzo's best-known film, the satirical *Tales from the Late Shogunate* (aka *Not Long after Leaving Shinagawa*, Bakumatsu taiyo-den, 1957). Kawashima's comedies are tough and individualistic, and his influence was crucial to the younger director, something Imamura well remembered when he later wrote the biography of his mentor.

Like Oshima, however, Imamura is also concerned with being Japanese. He has been said 'to search for the essence of Japaneseness through his works',[45] and has himself declared: 'I want to make really human, Japanese, unsettling films.'[46] One can imagine what he would have made of Ozu's brand of Japaneseness. In fact, one knows, for Imamura worked as assistant on Ozu's *Early Summer* (Bakushu, 1951), *The Flavour of Green Tea over Rice* (Ochazuke no aji, 1953), and *Tokyo Story*. Of these experiences he has said: 'I wouldn't say I wasn't influenced by Ozu. I would say I didn't *want* to be influenced by him.' The two men are so different, however, that there was no question of any similarity in approach to film.

One obvious example of these differences is their treatment of women. In films such as *Insect Woman* (Nippon konchuki, 1963) and *Intentions of Murder* (Akai satsui, 1964) Imamura presents Japanese women in all ways the anti-thesis of those in the films of Ozu, Mizoguchi or Naruse. Not in the least tragic, these women reject all conventional morality, are unfazed by poverty, war, and exploitative men, and survive by pure instinct.

In the Imamura film Japan itself is amoral, chaotic. The hero of *The Pornographers* (Erogoto: Jinruigaku nyumon, 1966) convinces himself (and us) that in making pornography he is actually serving society's true interests. In *A Man Vanishes* (Ningen johatsu, 1967) Japan is so fragmented that a man literally and symbolically disappears, falls between the social cracks and is never seen again. In *Vengeance is Mine* (Fukushu suru wa ware ni ari, 1976) the amoral hero is also immortal: Japan is in such a state that his very bones refuse burial in it. And in *Black Rain* (Kuroi ame, 1989) his people fight through the greatest chaos of all time — the devastation of Hiroshima by the atom bomb — and somehow survive.

Living in this jungle which is Japan, Imamura becomes the anthropological film-maker who with a scientific detachment observes the natives; in fact, the subtitle of *The Pornographers* is 'An Introduction to Anthropology'. He approaches his characters with the skill of a documentarist and has indeed made many television documentaries, all of them as outspoken as his films.

In this interest Imamura is joined by a number of his contemporaries. Oshima has made quite a few documentaries, as has Hani Susumu. In *She and He* (Kanojo to kare, 1963), Hani was filming a document of urban apartment life and its alienating effects. He and his scenarist, Shimizu Kunio, followed no script: they wrote the lines as they went along and each set-up became a documentary-like affair.

*Death by Hanging* (Koshikei, 1968, Oshima Nagisa)
Adachi Masao, Toura Mitsuhiro, Komatsu Hosei, Sato Kei, Ishido Toshiro

*Eros Plus Massacre* (Eros purasu gyakusatsu, 1969, Yoshida Yoshishige)
Hosokawa Toshiyuki

Others who came from a documentary background included Teshigahara Hiroshi. In *Woman in the Dunes* (Suna no onna, 1964) he showed a concern for realistic detail and an anthropological attitude — the first shot compares the human protagonist to an insect — shared by Abe Kobo, who had written the novel on which the film was based and who had himself provided the script. Later works by Teshigahara, such as *Summer Soldiers* (Natsu no heitai, 1971) and even the opulent *Rikyu* (1989), display a rigorously realistic visual style and a coolly analytical sense of structure.

These and later documentarists have made the documentary an acknowledged part of the Japanese cinema. Ogawa Shinsuke's multi-film *The Front Line for the Liberation of Japan* (Nihon kaiho sensen, 1968) attacks the merger of government and big business in the construction of the Tokyo International Airport. Tsuchimoto Noriaki made *Minamata: The Victims and Their World* (Minamata-kanja-san to sono sekai, 1971) about the worst pollution disaster in modern Japan, a film which had the effect of alerting the media and bringing the guilty company to court. Haneda Sumiko, Japan's finest woman documentarist, made the beautiful *Pale Grey Cherry Blossoms* (Usuzumi no sakura, 1986). In the four-hour *Magino Village* (Magino-mura, 1986) Ogawa lovingly describes a Japanese rural community. And Himeda Tadayoshi chronicles the destruction of such a small community by a new dam in his *Okumiomote: A Mountain Village* (Echigo Okumiomote, 1987–8).

Another documentarist turned feature film-maker was Yoshida Yoshishige, who shared a common *taiyozoku* background with Oshima and Shinoda, his contemporaries at Shochiku. He too was early drawn toward the

films of the *nouvelle vague* and emulated Godard's mixture of political polemic and personal vision. This is most
evident in *Eros Plus Massacre* (Erosu purasu gyakusatsu,
1969), a supremely dialectical film where 'documentary is
juxtaposed with fiction, Marx with Freud, history with
myth, politics with sexuality'.[47] The film, Yoshida's
'answer' to the work of Ozu, Kurosawa, Kinoshita and
Ichikawa, is, as the director suggests, to be defined nega-
tively, by what it is not. And it is not a traditional film. At
the same time it is very Japanese and Yoshida is not
unaware of traditional influences. 'Just as the last half of
*Ikiru* is concentrated on the . . . discussion of the deceased
Watanabe, so [my picture] focuses on contemporary per-
sons who act, thinking of the dead.'[48]

Herein lies one of the qualities of these new films of the
1960s: their innovative combination of both radical and
traditional means. Though, with Western styles now so
much a part of the Japanese cinema, it is often impossible
to determine, for example, whether the compositional
decentring of a scene is to be traced to the Japanese *ukiyo-e*,
the pictures of Mizoguchi, or the films of Michelangelo
Antonioni.

Shinoda Masahiro, also both a *taiyozoku* and a New
Wave director, continues to show influences from traditional Japanese film. In 1956 he saw and admired Ichikawa's adaptation of Izumi Kyoka's *Nihombashi*, a romantic and traditional story already once filmed by Mizoguchi.
It was to this world of romance and tradition that he
eventually returned. Before this, however, he carried out
thematic and stylistic experiments in such pictures as *Pale
Flower* (Kawaita hana, 1962), an Ishihara Shintaro story
about gangsters, and *Assassination* (Ansatsu, 1964), a
Yamada Nobuo script based on a Shiba Ryotaro story. In

*Assassination*, a *jidaigeki* purposely disjointed, the fragmented narrative serves to intensify the questioning of
conventional morality.

In his later films Shinoda returned to a tradition of
extreme aestheticism and to adaptations of literary works
by such 'officially' Japanese authors as Kawabata, Endo Shusaku, and the Edo playwright Chikamatsu Monzaemon.
His adaptation of one of the latter's Bunraku plays might
be contrasted with such filmed doll-dramas as Mizoguchi's
elegiac *A Story from Chikamatsu*, and Masumura's noisy
and vital *Love-Death at Sonezaki* (Sonezaki shinju, 1978), a
*michiyuki* film featuring a pop rock star.

Shinoda's *Double Suicide* (Shinju ten no Amijima, 1969),
on the other hand, uses the theatrical form itself in the
telling. Indeed, it opens with Shinoda himself in the Bunraku theatre making the film we are seeing, a device which
provides a theatrical framework. We are told the story;
one-shot one-scene methods are used (the finished film has
fewer than two hundred and fifty shots in it); and the
completely theatrical artificiality of the doll-drama is insisted upon, including the use of black-robed puppeteers
with live actors. Shinoda told Sato Tadao that these *kuroko*
are as much a part of his film as they are of the play, that
they 'serve as agents for the viewer who wants to penetrate
the truth of the lovers' plight'. They also represent Chikamatsu himself who, in this modern reading of the play
'created this anti-social world, tinged with the melo-
dramatic concept of a double suicide'.[49]

'Official' Japan is here criticized, but it is criticized on its
own terms. This is something which Shinoda may well
have learned from the films of Mizoguchi, films he very
much admires, *engeki-teki* though they may be. He himself
never worked with Mizoguchi but he did serve as assistant
director under Ozu, on *Tokyo Twilight* (Tokyo boshoku,

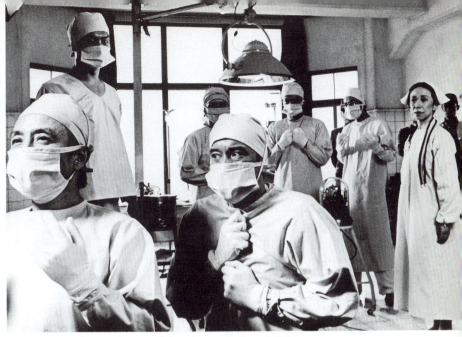

*The Sea and Poison* (Umi to dokuyaku, 1986, Kumai Kei)
Tamura Takahiko, Watanabe Ken, Kishida Kyoko

*Black Rain* (Kuroi ame, 1989, Imamura Shohei)
Kitamura Kazuo, Tanaka Yoshiko, Ozawa Shoichi

1958). Like Ozu and Mizoguchi, he was not interested in reality for its own sake. That, he declares, 'is not what interests me.... I begin with reality and see what higher idea comes out of it.'[50]

As did Mizoguchi himself. The older director thus remains Shinoda's inspiration, as he does to a number of younger Japanese directors. Shinoda has even compared Mizoguchi with Eisenstein and found the Russian wanting. 'The portrait of Oharu's despairing flight through the bamboo grove [in *The Life of Oharu*] conveys as much of the tragedy of the human condition as any film ever made. I don't know the exact length of the Odessa-steps sequence in *Potemkin*, but this example of Mizoguchi's one-scene one-cut technique is in no way inferior to the impact achieved in the few moments of Eisenstein's montage.'[51]

Shinoda's most Mizoguchi-like film, among others marked by a return to traditional styles, is *Banished Orin* (Hanare goze Orin, 1977), about a blind *samisen* player and her Oharu-like downfall. Others of the New Wave have shown a like disposition to tradition. Yoshida's *Wuthering Heights* (Arashigaoka, 1988), the Brontë novel in a period setting, is mainly concerned with aestheticism and thus joins many other films which return to a self-conscious Japaneseness after a period of foreign-inspired experimentation.

Following the various innovations of the 1960s and the gradual accommodations of the New Wave directors, it would have been appropriate for another new wave of young directors to appear in the 1980s had the finances of the motion-picture industry made this possible.

But they did not. Cinema's missing audience, debauched by television, never returned. Japan's enormous film factories (Toho, Shochiku, Toei) could not adjust themselves to a minority audience, and continued to pine for the missing majority. They attempted to woo them back with remakes, soft-core porno, 'youth' films and other such faltering genres. Directors and writers with new and original ideas were not encouraged. Those making the youth films of the 80s had, it is said, an average age of 65.

What had happened is typified by the fate of even such a popular genre as the *yakuza* film. With the *jidaigeki* fading into television, this modern descendant of the *matatabi-mono* became for a time the leading action-film genre. It has been noted that the *yakuza* code is really a parody of the samurai[52] and its expression is actually a continuation of the 'Chushingura mentality',[53] and so a lasting popularity seemed assured.

Stylistically conservative, the genre was indeed a completely 'rationalized' product in that it was constructed of standard units (the 'return' scene, the 'identification' scene, the 'reconciliation' scene), most of which were shot, from film to film, in identical fashion. These pictures were indeed Japanese in that each was constructed in the manner of traditional Japanese architecture: one module combined with another. Also Japanese was the way in which this routine product returned the audience to the early days when Matsunosuke insisted upon one duel in every reel.

And yet the popularity of the genre lasted only a decade (1963–73). There are various reasons why it was so short-lived. 'Modern *yakuza* heroes were models of submission and quite unlike American film gangsters' which the audience was flocking to see; also 'the sacrifice of individual desire for the sake of the group — the message inherent in the ritualistic *yakuza* film'[54] was of less interest to a more permissive and more moneyed younger audience. Though company producers for a time forced directors to keep churning out the product, the genre itself died.

Given such disheartening conditions, most directors fled their various companies. Responsibility had been taken from them and given to company producers, most of whom were interested only in whether or not a film made money. Few did, and as a consequence distrust of the new and the original became even more intense.

The result was a plethora of nudity, teenage heroes, science-fiction monsters, animated cartoons, and pictures about cute animals. There were exceptions, of course, among them the films of Yamada Yoji. This director had financially saved Shochiku with his popular series (some forty films by now) about the lovable Tora-san, country bumbler in the big city. These pictures, appearing under the generic title of *It's Tough Being a Man* (Otoko wa tsurai yo), are probably among the last of the *shomingeki*. And since Tora-san is a distant relative of Kihachi, a famous early Ozu character in such films as *A Story of Floating Weeds* (Ukigusa monogatari, 1934), there is a faint echo of traditional Japan as well.

Even Japan's finest directors were forced to look outside their companies, sometimes even outside the country, for financing. Kurosawa wandered the world to find foreign money to make *Dersu Uzala* (1975), *Kagemusha* (1980), *Ran* (1985) and *Dreams* (1989). With directors of this eminence forced to beg, it was impossible for young, untried directors to work within the Japanese industry at all unless they were willing to make the kind of products favoured by the company. The only way to create films of substance was to become independent.

This phenomenon had been observed in many countries and indeed most of the best cinema is now everywhere independently produced. In Japan, however, the growth of independent companies was relatively slow. There was initially only one such company to help new and even established directors. This was the Art Theatre Guild, which co-produced many of the films of Oshima, Hani, Shinoda, Yoshida, and the best film of Okamoto Kihachi, *Human Bullets* (Nikudan, 1968) and of Kuroki Kazuo, *Preparations for the Festival* (Matsuri no jumbi, 1975). At the same time other young directors have been able to find alternative financing.

Oguri Kohei, for example, made *Muddy River* (Doro no kawa, 1981) with money borrowed from a small iron foundry, the president of which was a film enthusiast. A black-and-white film set in Osaka in the 1950s, it was a deliberate return to the *shomingeki*, to traditional values. A small boy grows up and learns the disillusioning facts of life — a theme familiar to Japanese cinema since Ozu's *I Was Born, But. . . .* This thoughtful film found no local distribution at all until it had won several foreign prizes. It was then picked up by Toei and shown in their theatres, where it actually made money.

The success of *Muddy River* encouraged other companies to help finance the making of films. The Art Theatre Guild had already assisted such personal films as Higashi Yoichi's *Third Base* (Saado, 1978) and Negishi Yoshitaro's *Far Thunder* (Enrai, 1981), one an honest, unheroic story about a young delinquent, the other an unsentimental, humorous look at the rural proletariat. With the minority-audience success of these 'art' films, the ATG went on to help with the enormously successful *Family Game* (Kazoku geimu, 1984), Morita Yoshimitsu's satirical film about the new Japanese family. Based on the Honma Yohei novel, it showed the family members as education-crazed and geared only for success, in which process they had become, as indicated by the final sequence showing family sound asleep, quite dead.

One of the most important of the new young, independent directors was Yanagimachi Mitsuo whose *Farewell to the Land* (Saraba itoshiki daichi, 1982) is a powerful picture about Japan's despoiled countryside and the demoralized young. In 1985 he made one of the finest of the new independent films in *Fire Festival* (Hi matsuri), based on a Nakagami Kenji script and financed by one of Japan's largest department-store chains. In this film the young hero, a typically contemporary macho male, meets (both metaphorically and in reality) with the spirit of old Japan — with catastrophic results.

The themes of these new films are quite different from those of the bland fare served up by the major studios. Kumai Kei had for years wanted to make a film of *The Sea and Poison* (Umi to dokuyaku,) a novel by Endo Shusaku about the vivisection performed by the Japanese medical authorities on American prisoners-of-war. The major companies would have nothing to do with such a potentially explosive subject and Kumai finally obtained funding from the forward-looking production company, Herald-Ace. In 1986 the film appeared on all the best-film lists, made a profit, and was widely shown abroad.

Equally unsuitable, from the film industry's viewpoint, was a documentary by Hara Kazuo, based on a project by Imamura Shohei. *The Emperor's Naked Army Marches On* (Yuki yukite shingun, 1987) tells of a man determined to find out what happened to several of his wartime comrades, killed by their commanders after the war. His single-minded, even brutal investigation uncovers so much that there was even talk of the picture's not being released in Japan. It found a courageous distributor, however, in Image Forum, Japan's foremost experimental-film collective, and went on to play for months.

Also independent have been the films of Itami Juzo. The son of Itami Mansaku, the pre-war film director, and a well-known actor (he played the father in *Family Game*), Itami Juzo himself financed his first film, *The Funeral* (Ososhiki, 1985). It is a satire on the present-day Japanese who have lost so many of their own traditions: they can no longer sit in the Japanese fashion and have forgotten even such rituals as funeral rites. After the great success of this film Itami went on to make *Tampopo* (1986), a near-anthropological comedy about Japanese eating habits, and the two-part *A Taxing Woman* (Marusa no onna, 1987–8) about Japanese taxation procedures — a subject concerning which he said he learned much after the great financial success of *The Funeral*.

There is in the Itami picture a decided awareness of Japan, of Japaneseness. It is a matter which not only concerns the director but also becomes the subject of his satire. Itami is perceptive in his analysis of the differences between Japan and the West. 'Americans,' he has said, 'because of their ethnic, economic and educational differences, share far less in the way of common experience than do the Japanese ... living in Japan is like living in a nation of twins.' Western directors 'are the best storytellers ... they have to explain things, build up the details of a plot. A Japanese director can show a single image and know that the audience will immediately understand the meaning of time, place and background. That's why Japanese films ... seem so strange to foreigners.'[55]

The Japanese audience is certainly cognizant of being Japanese, but more and more young directors are seeking to redefine this quality. The young Somai Shinji made *Typhoon Club* (Taifu kurabu, 1986) after a Kato Yuji script which shows Japanese teenagers as they really are, not as the 'youth' pictures would have them. Kaneko Shusuke made the romantic, androgynous and deeply Japanese

*Summer Vacation: 1999* (1999-nen no natsu yasumi, 1988) in which the four adolescent boys are played by four adolescent girls. Hayashi Kaizo wrote, scripted and directed his first film, *To Sleep so as to Dream* (Yume miruyoni nemuritai, 1987), which is a deliberate return to the Japanese cinema of 1918, to the period of *The Glow of Life* and Japan's first actress. The picture is about this actress, now grown old and searching for the character she played in that picture, a search which runs through the gamut of Japanese film styles of the 1920s and 30s and in so doing encapsulates how Japanese films of those decades look to a young director at the end of the 1980s.

By now Japanese film style, like Japan itself, has become in many ways internationalized. Wave after wave of influences and techniques from international cinema have been digested and put to uses felicitous or otherwise. At the same time, new films continue to contain elements of earlier styles, either unconsciously or as pastiche, as nostalgia, as homage.

In *Typhoon Club*, for example, the director shoots the climactic dance scene in the eye of the typhoon from a great distance and holds it for a long time. One remembers the heroine alone by the solitary tree in Tanaka Eizo's *Living Corpse*, made as long ago as 1917. It is not impossible that Tanaka, if he were to direct *Typhoon Club*, might have elected to film this emotionally charged scene in precisely this manner.

In *The Funeral*, another example, the interiors are photographed straight on, Ozu-fashion, with great areas of space at the top. The scenes which make up *Fire Festival* are elliptical: the story is only one of several narrative strands, perhaps even the least important in that its conclusion is never explained. *Family Game* is pure presentation: the family members are shown as stereotypes, the house itself is seen as a movie set, and at the end the picture shifts so easily to allegory that one realizes it was parabolic from the beginning.

It might appear that, in this sense, young Japanese film-makers have reverted to a more 'Japanese' style. However, the majority of the current new directors have had little film training (many indeed come from television studios) and are not at all familiar with Japanese cinema of the past. Nor do they usually think of creating any specifically Japanese film style. The elements they employ are now a part of the international film vocabulary. They are no longer based on very different unspoken assumptions or unexamined premises; they are no longer so very different.

At the same time predilections, unexamined, often unnoticed, remain: a way of scripting, a way of composing a scene, a way of shooting, which is unmistakably Japanese. It is this Japanese way of ordering things, of choosing things, of creating things, and of revealing assumptions which no amount of internationalism can altogether suppress.

The history of Japanese cinema is, then, much like the history of Japan itself. Both are stories of a general adoption and a gradual adaptation to native needs. A century has passed since the beginnings of the cinema in Japan. And as the age of the film turns into the age of the video-tape and a new era of economic expansion opens for Japan, this cinema, originally an import from the West, remains an amalgam, one which is much enriched by foreign influences and which at the same time represents the traditionally Japanese.

# Notes

1. Ozu Yasujiro, *Kinema Jumpo*, June, 1958. Cited: Schrader, Leonard, ed., *The Masters of the Japanese Film*, unpublished ms., 1972.

2. Tanizaki Jun'ichiro, *Childhood Years: A Memoir*, trans. Paul McCarthy, Tokyo: Kodansha International, 1988, p. 97.

3. Yoshida Chieo, *Mo Hitotsu no Eiga-shi*. Cited: Sato Tadao, *Nihon Eiga Rironshi*, partial unpublished translation, Peter B. High, Tokyo: Hyronsha, 1977.

4. Ozu Yasujiro, *Watashi no Shonen Jidai*, essay, Tokyo: Makishoten, 1977. Cited: Schrader, *op. cit.*, p. 242.

5. Sato Tadao, *Currents in Japanese Cinema*, trans. Gregory Barrett, Tokyo: Kodansha International, 1982, p. 7.

6. Richie, Donald, 'Viewing Japanese Films', *Cinema and Cultural Identity*, ed. Wimal Dissanayake, London: University Press of America, 1988, p. 20.

7. Boardwell, David, and Kristin Thompson, 'Space and Narrative in the Films of Ozu', *Screen*, 17/2, 1976. Cited: Desser, David, *Eros Plus Massacre: An Introduction to the Japanese New Wave Cinema*, Bloomington: Indiana University Press, 1988, p. 17.

8. Nagai Kafu, 'A Strange Tale from East of the River' (1936), trans. Edward Seidensticker, *Kafu the Scribbler*, Stanford University Press, 1965, p. 278.

9. Kurosawa Akira, *Something Like an Autobiography*, trans. Audie Bock, New York: Knopf, 1982, p. 73.

10. Ozu Yasujiro. *Kinema Jumpo*, March, 1952. Cited: Schrader, *op. cit.*, p. 219.

11. Anderson, Joseph, and Donald Richie, *The Japanese Film: Art and Industry*, Tokyo: Tuttle, 1959, revised: Princeton University Press, 1982, p. 59.

12. Susukita Rokuhei. Quoted: Tanaka Jun'ichiro, *Nihon Eiga Hattushi*. Cited: Peter B. High, 'Japanese Film and the Great Kanto Earthquake of 1923', Nagoya: Daigaku Press, 1985.

13. Thornton, Sybil, *The Japanese Period Film: Rhetoric, Religion, Realism*, work-in-progress, unpublished ms., 1989.

14. Shinoda Masahiro. Cited: Schrader, *op. cit.,* p. 112.

15. Itami Mansaku. Cited: Sato Tadao, *Currents in Japanese Cinema*, trans. Gregory Barrett, Tokyo: Kodansha International, 1982, p. 34.

16. Boardwell, David, *Narrative in the Fiction Film*, Madison: University of Wisconsin Press, 1986, p. 150.

17. Shimazu Yasujiro. Quoted: Sato, *Nihon Eiga Rironshi*, partrial unpublished translation, Peter B. High, Tokyo: Hyronsha, 1977.

18. Yamanaka Sadao. Quoted: *ibid*.

19. Sugiyama Heiichi, *Eiga Kosei-ron*, 1941. Cited: *ibid.*

20. Kurosawa Akira. *Kinema Jumpo*, April, 1964. Cited: Schrader, *op. cit.*

21. Mizoguchi Kenji. Quoted Donald Richie. Cited: Schrader, *op. cit.*, p. 2.

22. Yoda Yoshitaka. *Kinema Jumpo*, April, 1961. Cited: Schrader, *op. cit.*, p. 97.

23. Shinoda Masahiro. Quoted: Schrader, *op. cit.*, p. 20.

24. Iwasaki Akira. *Kinema Jumpo*, February, 1963. Cited: Schrader, *op. cit.*, p. 281.

25. Sato Tadao, *Nihon Eiga Shishoi*, Tokyo: Tokyo Shoten, 1970. Cited: High, Peter, B., 'Japanese Film and the Great Kanto Earthquake of 1923', Nagoya: Daigaku Press, 1985.

26. Burch, Nöel, *To the Distant Observer: Form and Meaning in the Japanese Cinema*, Berkeley: University of California Press, 1979, p. 195–7.

27. Richie, Donald, '*Humanity and Paper Balloons*: Some Remarks on Structure', New Delhi: *Cinemaya*, 2/1, 1989.

28. Iwasaki Akira. Quoted: Schrader, *op. cit.*, p. 422.

29. Iwasaki Akira. Quoted: Sato Tadao, *Nihon Eiga Rironshi*, partial, unpublished translation, Peter B. High, Tokyo: Hyronsha, 1977.

30. Kurosawa Akira. Quoted: *ibid.*

31. Rimer, J. Thomas, *Pilgrimages: Aspects of Japanese Literature and Culture*, Honolulu: University of Hawaii Press, 1988, pp. x, 1113.

32. Andrew, Dudley, in *International Directory of Films and Filmmakers: Directors*, ed. Christopher Lyon, London: Macmillan, 1984, p. 376.

33. Boardwell, David, in *ibid.*, p. 398.

34. Naruse Mikio. *Kinema Jumpo*, April, 1962. Cited: Schrader, *op. cit.*, p. 343.

35. Sato Tadao, *Ozu Yasujiro no Geijutsu*, Tokyo: Asahi Shimbun-sha, 1971. Cited: Schrader, *op. cit.*, p. 301.

36. Bock, Audie, *Mikio Naruse*, unfinished, unpublished ms., n.d.

37. Naruse Mikio. *Kinema Jumpo*, April, 1960. Cited: Schrader, *op. cit.*, p. 364.

38. Anderson, Joseph L., 'Japanese Film', *Kodansha Encyclopedia of Japan*, Tokyo: Kodansha International, 1983: Vol. 2, p. 273.

39. Oshima Nagisa. Quoted: Sato Tadao, *Currents in Japanese Cinema*, trans. Gregory Barrett, Tokyo: Kodansha International, 1982, p. 213.

40. Oshima Nagisa. Quoted: *ibid*, p. 213.

41. Oshima Nagisa. Quoted: Iwasaki Akira, *Sekai no Eiga Saka: Oshima, Kinema Jumpo*, 1970. Cited: McDonald, Keiko, *Cinema East*, London: Associated University Press, 1983, p. 125.

42. Sato Tadao, *Currents in Japanese Cinema*, trans. Gregory Barrett, Tokyo: Kodansha International, 1982.

43. Imamura Shohei. Quoted: Bock, Audie, *Japanese Film Directors*, Tokyo: Kodansha International, 1978, p. 309.

44. Richie, Donald, 'Notes for a Study on Shohei Imamura', Sydney/ Melbourne: Australian Film Institute, 1983, p. 38.

45. Imamura Shohei. Quoted: Rikiya Tayama, *Nihon no Eiga Sakkatachi: Sosaku no Himitsu*, Tokyo: Davido-sha, 1975. Cited: Bock, *op. cit.*, p. 288.

46. Imamura Shohei. Quoted: Sugiyama Hiichi, *Imamura Shohei ron*, Tokyo: *Kinema Jumpo*, 1975. Cited Bock, *op. cit.*, p. 289.

47. Desser, David, *Eros Plus Massacre: An Introduction to the Japanese New Wave Cinema*, Bloomington: Indiana University Press, 1988, p. 200.

48. Yoshida, Yoshishige. Quoted: Sato Tadao, *Kurosawa Akira eiga taikai*, Tokyo: *Kinema Jumpo*, 1971. Cited: McDonald, *op. cit.*, p. 172.

49. Shinoda Masahiro. Quoted: Sato Tadao, *Nihon Eiga Shishoi*, partial, unpublished translation, Peter B. High, Tokyo: Tokyo Shoten, 1970.

50. Shinoda Masahiro. Quoted: Bock, *op. cit.*, p. 342.

51. Shinoda Masahiro. Quoted, Schrader, *op. cit.*, p. 25.

52. De Vos, George A., *Socialization of Achievement: Essays on the Cultural Psychology of the Japanese*, Berkeley/Los Angeles: University of California Press, 1975. Quoted: Barrett, Gregory, *Archetypes in Japanese Film*, Selinsgrove: Susquehanna University Press, 1989, p. 64.

53. Buruma, Ian, *A Japanese Mirror: Heroes and Villains of Japanese Culture*, London: Jonathan Cape, 1984. Quoted: Barrett, *op. cit.*, p. 64.

54. Barrett, Gregory, *op. cit.*, p. 64.

55. Itami Juzo. Quoted: Canby, Vincent, *The New York Times Magazine*, 18 June 1989.

# Glossary

| | |
|---|---|
| *benshi* | film commentator, lecturer, compère — a master of ceremonies whose appearance was an assumed part of early Japanese film showings |
| Bunraku | the Japanese puppet drama which attained artistic maturity in the eighteenth century |
| *chambara* | sword fights in plays and films, later generic term for low-class samurai pictures |
| *engeki-teki* | 'stage-like', usually pejorative |
| *furukusai* | 'old-fashioned', usually pejorative |
| *gendaigeki* | generic term for films about contemporary life |
| *gidayu* | a kind of narrative chant (*joruri*) which greatly influenced Kabuki music, though originated for the Bunraku |
| *haha-mono* | generic term for films about mothers |
| *haiku* | a 17-syllable verse form consisting of three metrical units of 5, 7, and 5 syllables respectively |
| *ikebana* | 'living flowers', the Japanese art of flower arranging |
| *jidaigeki* | generic term for historical films, mainly those of the Tokugawa period (1615–1868) |
| *joruri* | narrative chant commonly associated with the Bunraku |
| Kabuki | one of the three major classical Japanese theatres (with Noh and Bunraku) which matured in the eighteenth century |
| *kagezerifu* | 'shadow dialogue', an early kind of film narration later developed by the *benshi* |
| *kanji* | ideographs, Chinese in origin, appropriated by the Japanese to form one component of the written language |

89

| | |
|---|---|
| *keiko-eiga* | films with definite (usually leftist) political overtones, sometimes loosely translated as 'tendency films' |
| *kodan* | didactic storytelling, much of the material drawn from Confucian interpretations of medieval war tales and historical events |
| *kowairo* | 'voice-colouring', the 'dubbing' of lines with full emotional emphasis used in early film presentations |
| *kurogo* | veiled, black–garbed stage assistant in Bunraku, and later in Kabuki |
| *kyuha* | 'old school', meaning Kabuki and used in opposition to *shimpa*, 'new school', the latter term becoming generic for a particular post-Kabuki kind of theatre |
| *matatabi-mono* | films about itinerant gamblers, ruffians, *yakuza* |
| *michiyuki* | the 'journey', a set piece in the Bunraku and Kabuki — the travellers are usually lovers |
| Noh | Japan's oldest extant theatre, originating in the fourteenth century; a form of dance-drama |
| *rakugo* | a popular form of comic monologue |
| *ronin* | 'floating men', masterless samurai |
| *samisen* | a three-stringed Japanese musical instrument, more frequently *shamisen* |
| *senikyoyo-eiga* | 'national policy films', the pre-war and wartime product made under government control |
| *shimpa* | 'new school', in opposition to the 'old school' of Kabuki; an intermediate theatrical form, partly Western |
| Shingeki | 'new theatre', comparable to that in Western countries, opposed to classical Japanese theatre and distinct from *shimpa* |
| Shinkokugeki | 'new national drama', off-shoot of Shingeki |

|               |                                                                                                              |
| ------------- | ------------------------------------------------------------------------------------------------------------ |
|               | and mainly concerned with historical drama, occasionally descending to *chambara*, now defunct               |
| *shomingeki*  | films about the lower middle classes                                                                         |
| *shoshimengeki* | serio-comedy of the salaried class                                                                         |
| *taiyozoku*   | 'sun tribe', late 1950s cult of fiction and films about rebellious youth                                      |
| *tatami*      | reed-covered straw matting in traditional Japanese room                                                       |
| *tsuma-mono*  | generic term for films about wives                                                                           |
| *ukiyo-e*     | 'pictures of the floating world', woodblock prints of Tokugawa period (1615–1868) devoted to the pleasures of Edo (Tokyo) |
| *yakuza*      | generic term for gangster, gambler, thug, good-for-nothing, etc.                                             |

# Bibliography

Anderson, Joseph L., 'Japanese Film', *Kodansha Encyclopedia of Japan*, Tokyo: Kodansha, Ltd, 1983.

Anderson, Joseph L., and Donald Richie, *The Japanese Film: Art and Industry*, Tokyo: Tuttle, 1959, revised: Princeton University Press, 1982.

Andrew, Dudley, 'Mizoguchi', *International Directory of Films and Filmmakers: Directors*, ed. Christopher Lyon, London: Macmillan, 1984.

Barrett, Gregory, *Archetypes in Japanese Film*, Selinsgrove: Susquehanna University Press, 1989.

Boardwell, David, *Narrative in the Fiction Film*, Madison: University of Wisconsin Press, 1986.

Boardwell, David, 'Ozu', *International Directory of Films and Filmmakers*, ed. Christopher Lyon, London: Macmillan, 1984.

Boardwell, David, *Ozu and the Poetics of Cinema*, Princeton University Press, 1988.

Bock, Audie, *Japanese Film Directors*, Tokyo: Kodansha International, 1978.

Bock, Audie, *Mikio Naruse*, Filmography, Film Center, Chicago Institute of Fine Arts, 1984.

Bock, Audie, *Mikio Naruse*, unfinished, unpublished ms., n.d.

Burch, Noël, *To the Distant Observer: Form and Meaning in the Japanese Cinema*, Berkeley: University of California Press, 1979.

Buruma, Ian, *A Japanese Mirror: Heroes and Villains of Japanese Culture*, London: Jonathan Cape, 1984.

Desser, David, *Eros Plus Massacre: An Introduction to the Japanese New Wave Cinema*, Bloomington: Indiana University Press, 1988.

De Vos, George A., *Socialization of Achievement: Essays on the Cultural Psychology of the Japanese*, Berkeley/Los Angeles: University of California Press, 1975.

92

High, Peter B., 'Japanese Film and the Great Kanto Earthquake of 1923', Nagoya: Daigaku Press, 1985.

Kurosawa Akira, *Something Like an Autobiography*, trans. Audie Bock, New York: Knopf, 1982.

McDonald, Keiko, *Cinema East*, London: Associated University Press, 1983.

McDonald, Keiko, *Mizoguchi*, Boston: Twayne Publishers, 1984.

Mellen, Joan, *Voices from the Japanese Cinema*, New York: Liveright, 1974.

Mellen, Joan, *The Waves at Genji's Door, New York: Pantheon*, 1976.

Nagai Kafu, *Kafu the Scribbler*, ed. and trans. E.G. Seidensticker, Stanford University Press, 1965.

Richie, Donald, *The Films of Akira Kurosawa*, Berkeley: University of California Press, 1965, expanded edition, 1985.

Richie, Donald, '*Humanity and Paper Balloons*: Some Remarks on Structure', New Delhi: *Cinememaya*, 2/1, 1989.

Richie, Donald, *Japanese Cinema: Film Style and National Character*, Garden City, New York: Doubleday Anchor Books, 1971.

Richie, Donald, *The Japanese Movie*, Tokyo: Kodansha, 1965, revised, 1981.

Richie, Donald, *Ozu*, Berkeley: University of California Press, 1974.

Richie, Donald, 'Notes for a Study on Shohei Imamura', Sydney/Melbourne: Australian Film Institute, 1983.

Richie, Donald, 'Viewing Japanese Films', *Cinema and Cultural Identity*, ed. Wimal Dissanayake, London: University Press of America, 1988.

Rimer, J. Thomas, *Pilgrimages: Aspects of Japanese Literature and Culture*, Honolulu: University of Hawaii Press, 1988.

Sato Tadao, *Currents in Japanese Cinema*, trans. Gregory Barrett, Tokyo: Kodansha International, 1982.

Sato Tadao, *Kurosawa Akira eiga taikai*, Tokyo: *Kinema Jumpo*, 1971.

Sato Tadao, *Nihon Eiga Rironshi*, partial, unpublished translation, Peter B. High, Tokyo: Hyronsha, 1977.

Sato Tadao, *Nihon Eiga Shishoi*, partial, unpublished translation, Peter B. High, Tokyo: Tokyo Shoten, 1970.

Sato Tadao, *Ozu Yasujiro no Geijitsu*, Tokyo: Asahi Shimbunasha, 1971.

Schrader, Leonard, ed., *The Masters of the Japanese Film*, unpublished ms, 1972.

Sugiyama Hiichi, *Imamura Shohei-ron*, Tokyo: Kinema Jumpo, 1975.

Tanizaki Jun'ichiro, *Childhood Years: A Memoir*, trans. Paul McCarthy, Tokyo: Kodansha International, 1988.

Thompson, Kristin, '*Late Spring* and Ozu's Unreasonable Style', *Breaking the Glass Armor*, Princeton University Press, 1988.

Thornton, Sybil, *The Japanese Period Film: Rhetoric, Religion, Realism*, work-in-progress, unpublished ms., 1989.

# Index

*Au bout de souffle*, 68
Abe Kobo, 74
*Actor's Revenge, An*, 60
Adauchi senshu, 33
*Affair at Kamakura*, 65
Ai no koriida, 67
Ai to kibo no machi, 65
Akai satsui, 72
Akibiyori, 50
Akutagawa Ryunosuke, 53
*All Quiet on the Western Front*, 37
*And Yet We Live*, 46
Anjo-ke no butokai, 43
Ansatsu, 75f
Antonioni, Michelangelo, 75
Arashigaoka, 78
Art Theatre Guild, 80
*Assassination*, 75f
*Autumn Afternoon, An*, 50

*Bad Boys*, 63
Bakumatsu taiyo-den, 71
Bakushu, 71
*Ball at the Anjo House, A*, 43
*Ballad of Narayama, The*, 56, 58
Bando Tsumasaburo, 20f, 38, 45
Bangiku, 52
*Banished Orin*, 78
Banshun, 49
*Battle of Kawanakajima, The*, 39
*benshi*, 3ff., 12, 17, 89
*Billionaire, A*, 45
Biruma no tategoto, 59
*Black Rain*, 72
Bluebird Productions, 26
Bokuto kidan, 58
Bonchi, 59
*Boy*, 67f.

*Boy Called Third Base, A*, see *Third Base*
*Broken Commandment, The*, 59
*Broken Drum, The*, 45
Brontë, Emily, 78
Bunraku, 2, 3, 76, 89

*Cabinet of Dr Caligari, The*, 24
*Carmen's Pure Love*, 45
*Cat, Shozo and Two Women, A*, 58
*Ceremony, The*, 67
Chabrol, Claude, 65
*chambara*, 53f., 89
Chaplin, Charles, 18
Chekhov, Anton, 10
Chichi ariki, 43
Chikamatsu Monzaemon, 4, 9, 55, 76
Chikamatsu monogatari, 49, 76
*Children of the Atom Bomb*, 46
*Children of the Beehive*, 46
*Chuji from Kunisada: A Flock of Wild Geese*, 18
*Chuji's Travel Diary*, 19
Chuji tabi nikki, 19
*Chushingura*, 8, 20, 39, 42, 55
*Cinématograph Lumière*, 1
*Civilization*, 5, 29
*Crazed Fruit*, 65
*Crossroads*, 23f.
*Crowded Streetcar, A*, 45
*Crucified Lovers, The*, 49, 76
*Cuckoo: A New Version, The*, 6

De Sica, Vittorio, 46
*Death by Hanging*, 67
*Dersu Uzala*, 80
Dobu no kawa, 81
Dodesukaden, 54

Dokkoi ikiteiru, 46
Double Suicide, 76
*Downfall of Osen, The*, 6
*Dreams*, 80
*Drunken Angel*, 46

*Early Spring*, 49
*Early Summer*, 71
*Earth*, 39
Echigo Okumi-Omote, 74
Edison Vitascope, 1
Eisenstein, Sergei, 48, 78
*Elegy to Violence*, 71
*Emperor's Naked Army Marches On, The*, 82
*Empire of the Senses*, 67
Endo Shusaku, 76, 82
Enjo, 59
Enrai, 81
*Erogoto: Jinryugaku nyumon*, 72
*Eros Plus Massacre*, 75
Eros purasu gyoakusatsu, 75
expressionism, 24

Fairbanks, Douglas, 21
*Family Game, The*, 81, 83f.
*Far Thunder*, 81
*Farewell to the Land*, 81
film, Japanese
  aesthetics, 7ff., 48; beginnings, 1ff.;
  early period films, 10ff.; early
  programming, 1ff.; early projection
  1ff.; early Shingeki-influenced
  films, 11ff.; flashbacks, 5ff.; genres,
  44–5, 79; independent production,
  78ff.; influence of foreign films,
  5ff., 14ff., 17–18, 21ff., 26f., 29ff.,
  38ff., 41ff., 43, 46, 54, 68; influence
  of theatre, 2ff., 10ff., 67f.; 'New
  Wave' films, 66ff., 75, 78;
  Occupation films, 41ff.; post-
  earthquake period films, 18ff.; post-
  earthquake period films, 18ff.; post-

earthquake modern-life films, 25ff.;
  post-earthquake social protest films,
  33ff.; postwar comedy, 45ff.;
  postwar documentary influence,
  60ff., 74; postwar modern-life
  films, 49ff.; postwar period films,
  48ff., 53f.; 'tendency films', 33f.;
  wartime films, 37ff.
*Fire Festival*, 82, 84
*Fires on the Plain*, 59
*Five Scouts*, 37
*Flavour of Green Tea over Rice, The*, 71
*Floating Clouds*, 52–3
*Floating Weeds*, 50
*Flowing*, 52
Ford, John, 18
*Front Line for the Liberation of Japan*, 74
Fuefukigawa, 58
Fukazawa Shichiro, 58
Fukushu suru wa ware ni ari, 72
*Funeral, The*, 83f.
Furumi Tạkuji, 33
Furuyo shonen, 63
Futagawa Buntaro, 20

Gance, Abel, 18
*Gate of Hell, The*, 24
Gembaku no ko, 46
*gendaigeki*, 17f, 25ff., 43ff., 49, 54, 71,
  89
*Generals, Staff and Soldiers*, 38
*Genroku Loyal Forty-seven Ronin, The*,
  39
*Giants and Toys*, 64–5
*gidayu*, 3, 89
Gion no shimai, 27–8
Gishiki, 67
*Glow of Life, The*, 12, 84
Godard, Jean-Luc, 65, 68, 75
Gomikawa Jumpei, 56
Gonin no sekkohei, 37
Gorky, Maxim, 11, 14
Gosho Heinosuke, 25f., 50f., 68

Griffith, D. W., 6, 12, 14, 46f.
*Growing Up*, 50

Hachi no su no kodomotachi, 46
Hadaka no shima, 63
*haha-mono*, 44, 89
*haiku*, 48, 89
Hakai, 59
Hakuchi, 54
Hakuchi no torima, 68–9
Hanagata senshu, 30
Hanare goze Orin, 78
Hanayaki Harumi, 12
Haneda Sumiko, 74
Hani Susumu, 63, 72, 81
Hara Kazuo, 82
Hara Setsuko, 45
Harakiri, 56
*Harp of Burma, The*, 59
Hart, William S., 21
Hasegawa Kazuo, 60
Hasegawa Shin, 19f.
Hashimoto Shinobu, 53f., 55
Hataraku ikka, 38
Hawaii-Marei oki kaisen, 38
Hayashi Fumiko, 52f.
Hayashi Kaizu, 84
Hearn, Lafcadio, 56
*Her Brother*, 59
Herald-Ace, 82
Hi matsuri, 81, 84
*Hidden Fortress, The*, 54
Higashi Yoichi, 81
Higuchi Ichiyo, 50, 55
Himeda Tadayoshi, 74
*History*, 39
Hitchcock, Alfred, 15
Honma Yohei, 81
Hosoyama Kiyomatsu, 11
*Human Bullets*, 81
*Human Condition, The*, 56
*Humanity and Paper Balloons*, 34–6

*I Am a Cat*, 59
*I Was Born, But . . .*, 29–30, 32, 81
Ibsen, Henrik, 10
Ichiban utsukushiku, 38
Ichikawa Kon, 8, 44f., 54, 58–9, 65, 67, 75
Ide Toshiro, 52
*Idiot, The*, 54
*ikebana*, 11, 89
Ikeru shikabane, 11
Ikiru, 4, 54, 75
Ikiru ningyo, 32
Image Forum, 82
Imai Tadashi, 44, 46, 55–6, 60
Imamura Shohei, 58, 67, 70ff., 82
Inagaki Hiroshi, 20
Ince, Thomas, 5
*Inn in Osaka, An*, 50
*Insect Woman*, 71–2
*Intentions of Murder*, 72
*Intolerance*, 14
*Iron Horse, The*, 18
Ishido Toshiro, 67
Ishihara Shintaro, 65, 75
Ishihara Yujiro, 65
*Island, The*, 63
Itami Juzo, 83
Itami Mansaku, 20–1, 33, 53f.
Ito Daisuke, 8, 19, 21, 23, 26, 28, 32f., 53, 60
Ito Sachio, 56
*It's Tough Being a Man*, 80
Iwasaki Akira, 29, 43f.
Izumi Kyoka, 75

*Japanese Tragedy, A*, 60
*jidaigeki*, 17ff., 32f., 42, 44, 53, 56, 60, 75, 79, 89
Jigokumon, 24
*Jirocho from Shimizu*, 19
*joruri*, 2, 89
Jujiro, 23–4

Kabuki, 3, 5, 6, 10, 24, 39, 58, 60, 89
Kachusha, 11
Kaeriyama norimasu, 12
Kagemusha, 24, 54, 80
*kagezerifu*, 4, 89
Kagi, 59
Kaidan, 56
Kaishain seikatsu, 25
*Kakita Akanishi*, 33, 54
Kakushi toride no san-akunin, 54
Kanajo to kare, 72
Kancho mada shizezu, 38
Kaneko Shusuke, 83
*kanji*, 48, 89
Karumen junjosu, 45
Kataoka Chiezu, 21
Kato Yuji, 83
*Katsusha*, 11
Kawabata Yasunari, 23, 76
Kawaita hana, 79
Kawanakajima kassen, 39
Kawashima Yuzo, 70f.
Kawatake Mokuami, 34
Kazoku geimu, 81
*keiko-eiga*, 33f., 46, 66, 90
Kenka ereji, 71
*Kentucky Cinderella, A*, 26
*Key, The*, 59
Kihachi, 80
Kikushima Ryuzo, 52, 54
Kinoshita Keisuke, 43f., 45, 56, 58, 60, 65, 75
Kinugasa Teinosuke, 23ff., 26, 39, 60
*Kisses*, 65
Kobayashi Masaaki, 20, 56
*Kochiyama Soshun*, 34
Koda Aya, 59
*kodan*, 3, 19, 23, 90
Kokoro, 59
Kokushi muso, 33
Koshikei, 67
*kowairo*, 4, 90
Kuchizuki, 65

Kumai Kei, 82
Kunieda Kenji, 42
Kunisada Chuji: Kare no mure, 18
*kurogo*, 76, 90
Kuroi Ame, 72
Kuroki Kazuo, 81
Kurosawa Akira, 4, 6, 8, 17f., 20, 24, 38f., 41, 43f., 45f., 53–4, 66f., 75, 80
Kurutta kajitsu, 65
Kurutta ippeiji, 23–4
Kutsukake Tokijiro, 19–20
Kwaidan, 56
Kyo Machiko, 45
Kyojin to gangu, 64–5
*Kyoya Collar Shop, The*, 24, 32
Kyoya erimise, 24, 32
*kyuha*, 10, 68, 90

Lang, Fritz, 18
*Late Autumn*, 50
*Late Chrysanthemums*, 52
*Late Spring*, 49
*Life of an Office Worker, The*, 25
*Life of Oharu, The*, 48f., 78
*Live Doll, A*, 32
*Living Corpse*, 11, 84
*Love-Death at Sonezaki*, 76
*Lower Depths, The*, 14
*Loyal Forty-seven Ronin, The*, 8, 20, 39, 43, 55
Lubitsch, Ernst, 15, 18, 29, 52, 68

Machi no hitobito, 25
*Magino Village*, 74
Magino mura, 74
Ma-in densha, 45
Makino Masahiro, 20, 33, 60, 68
Makino Shozo, 10, 18f., 20
*Man-Slashing, Horse-Piercing Sword*, 21, 33
*Man Vanishes, A*, 72

*Man Who Left His Will on Film, The*, 68

*Marital Relations*, 58

*Marriage Circle, The*, 18

Marusa no onna, 83

Masumura Yasuzo, 64–5, 76

Matatabi, 60

*matatabi-mono*, 19f., 60, 79, 90

Matsunosuke, see Onoe Matsunosuke

Matsuri no jumbi, 81

Maupassant, Guy de, 17

*Max Mon Amour*, 68

Meoto zensai, 58

Meshi, 52

*Metropolitan Symphony*, 32

*michiyuki*, 58, 76, 90

Mifune Toshiro, 45

*Minamata: The Victims and Their World*, 74

Minamata-kanja-san to sono sekai, 74

Mishima, Yukio, 59

*Miyamoto Musashi*, 55

Mizoguchi, Kenji, 6, 8, 27ff., 32, 39, 43, 48f., 53, 55, 64, 67, 72, 75

Mizuki Yoko, 53

Mori Masayuki, 45

Mori Ogai, 49

Morita Yoshimitsu, 81

*Morning with the Osone Family, A*, 43

*Most Beautiful, The*, 38

*Mr Pu*, 45

*Mud and Soldiers*, 37

*Muddy River*, 81

*Muddy Waters*, 55

Mura no sensei, 25

Murata Minoru, 12ff., 15

Murasaki zukin: ukiyo-e shi, 18

Nagai Kafu, 17, 58

Nagatsuka Takashi, 39

Nagereru, 52

Nakagami Kenji, 82

Nakahira Ko, 65

Narayama bushiko, 56, 58

Naruse Mikio, 30, 38, 52f., 54, 72

Natsu no Heitai, 74

Natsume Soseki, 39, 59

Naze kanajo o so saseta ka, 32–3

Negishi Yoshitaro, 81

Nekko, Shozo to futari no onna, 58

*Nibelungen, Die*, 18

Nichiyobi, 25

*Night and Fog in Japan*, 66, 68

*Night Drum*, 55

Nigorie, 55

Nihon kaihi senzen, 74

Nihon no higeki, 60

Nihon no yoru to kiri, 66, 68

Nihombashi, 75

Nikudan, 81

1999 — nen no natsu yasumi, 84

Ningen johatsu, 72

Nijuyon no hitomi, 56

Ningen no jokken, 56

Ninjo kami fusen, 34–6

Nippon konchuki, 71f.

Nishizumi senshacho-den, 38

*No Regrets for Our Youth*, 43, 66f.

Nobi, 59

Noda Kogo, 49, 55

Nogiku no gotoki kimi nariki, 56

Noh, 2, 6, 70, 90

Nomura Hotei, 18f.

Nora inu, 46

*Not Long after Leaving Shinagawa*, 71

Ochazuke no aji, 71

Oda Sakunosuke, 58

*Odd Obsession*, 59

Ogawa Shinsuke, 74

Oguni Hideo, 54

Ogura Kohei, 81

Okamoto Kihachi, 81

Okochi Denjiro, 19f., 21

*Okumi-Omote: A Mountain Village*, 74

Okuman choja, 45

*One Wonderful Sunday*, 46
*Onna ga kaidan o agaru toki*, 52
Onoe Matsunosuke, 10, 18, 21, 53, 68, 79
Ooka Shohei, 59
*Orizuri osen*, 6
*Orochi*, 20
*Osaka no yado*, 50
Osanai Kaoru, 12, 15, 60
Oshima Nagisa, 8, 65ff., 74, 85
*Osone-ke no asa*, 43
*Ososhiki*, 83
*Otoko wa tsurai yo*, 80
*Ototo*, 58
*Our Neighbour, Miss Yae*, 30
*Outcast, The*, 59
Ozu, Yasujiro, 5, 8, 18, 25f., 28ff., 32, 39, 43, 49f., 53, 55, 64, 67f., 70, 72, 75f., 81, 84

*Page of Madness, A*, 23–4
*Page Out of Order, A*, 23–4
*Pale Flower*, 75
*Pale Grey Cherry Blossoms*, 74
*Peerless Patriot*, 33
Pickford, Mary, 14
*Pornographers, The*, 72
*Potemkin*, 78
*Preparations for the Festival*, 81
*Pu-san*, 45
*Purple Hood: Woodblock Artist, The*, 18

*Ran*, 24, 54, 80
*Rashomon*, 6, 53
*Rekishi*, 39
*Repast*, 52
*Revenge Champion*, 33
*Rikyu*, 74
*River Fuefuki, The*, 58
*Rojo no reikon*, 12, 14–15, 24, 32
*ronin*, 20, 33, 54, 90
*Roningai*, 20
Rossellini, Roberto, 46

*Roue, La*, 18

*Saado*, 81
*Saikaku Ibara*, 48
*Saikaku ichidai onna*, 48f.
*Samma no aji*, 50
*Sanjuro*, 54
*Sanshiro Sugata*, 39
*Sansho daiyu*, 49
*Sansho the Bailiff*, 49
*Saraba itoshi daichi*, 81
Sasaki Mamoru, 67
Sato Tadao, 6, 52, 68, 76
*Sazen Tange: The Million Ryo Pot*, 54
Schmitzbaum, Wilhelm, 14
*Sea and Poison, The*, 82
*Season of the Sun*, 65
Sei no kagayaki, 12
Sekigawa Hideo, 60
*senikyoyo-eiga*, 37f., 90
*Seppuku*, 56
*Seven Samurai*, 54
*She and He*, 72
*She Was Like a Wild Chrysanthemum*, 56
Shiba Ryotaro, 75
*Shichinin no samurai*, 54
Shimazaki Toso, 59
Shimazu Yasujiro, 25f., 30, 50
Shimizu Hiroshi, 30f., 45, 60
Shimizu Kunio, 72
*Shimizu no Jirocho*, 19
*shimpa*, 5, 10, 90
*shin jidaigeki*, 18
Shindo Kaneto, 44, 46, 63
*Shingeki*, 10ff., 18, 70, 90
*Shinju ten no Amijima*, 76
Shinkokugeki, 18, 90–1
Shinoda Masahiro, 21, 28, 67, 74, 76f., 81
Shirasaka Yoshio, 65
*Shogun to sambo to hei*, 38
*shomingeki*, 25ff., 50, 71, 80, 91

Shonen, 67
*Sisters of the Gion*, 27f., 53
Somai Shinji, 83
Sonezaki shinju, 76
*Souls on the Road*, 12, 14–15, 24, 32
*Southern Justice*, 26
*Spy Isn't Yet Dead, The*, 38
*Star Athlete, A*, 30
*Story from Chikamatsu, A*, 49, 76
*Story of Floating Weeds, A*, 80
*Story of Tank Commander Nishizumi, The*, 38
*Stray Dog*, 46
*Street of Masterless Samurai, The*, 20, 33
Subarashiki nichiyobi, 46
Sugata Sanshiro, 39
Sugiyama Heiichi, 26
*Summer Soldiers*, 74
*Summer Vacation: 1999*, 84
Suna no onna, 74
*Sunday*, 25
Susukita Rokuhei, 18ff., 20ff., 34
Suzuki Seijun, 71
Suzuki Sugiyoshi, 32f.

Taguchi Tetsu, 38
Taifu kurabu, 83
Taiyo no kisetsu, 55
*taiyozoku*, 65, 74f., 91
Takamine Hideko, 45
Takekurabe, 50
Takeyama Michio, 59
*Tale from East of the River, A*, 58
*Tale of Genji, The*, 55
*Tales from the Late Shogunate*, 71
Tampopo, 83
Tamura Tsutomu, 67
Tanaka Eizo, 11f., 25, 84
Tanaka Kinuyo, 45
Tanaka Sumie, 52
Tange Sazen — Hyakuman ryo no tsubo, 54
Tanikawa Shuntaro, 60

Tanizaki Jun'ichiro, 1–2, 58f.
Tasaka Tomotaka, 37
Tati, Jacques, 32
*Taxing Woman, A*, 83
*Temple of the Gold Pavilion, The*, 59
Teshigahara Hiroshi, 74
*There Was a Father*, 43
*They Who Tread on the Tiger's Tail*, 41f.
*Third Base*, 81
*To Sleep so as to Dream*, 84
Tokai kokyogaku, 32
*Tokijiro from Kutsukake*, 19f.
Tokyo boshoku, 76
*Tokyo Drifter*, 71
Tokyo koshinkyoku, 32
*Tokyo March*, 32
Tokyo mongatari, 50, 71
Tokyo nagaremono, 71
Tokyo saiban, 56
Tokyo sensen sengo hiwa, 68
*Tokyo Story*, 50, 71
*Tokyo Trial, The*, 56
*Tokyo Twilights*, 76
Tolstoy, Leo, 11
Tonari no Yae-chan, 30
Tora no o o fumu otokotachi, 41f.
Tora-san, 80
*Townspeople*, 25
*Town of Love and Hope, A*, 65
Toyoda Shiro, 58
*Troubled Waters*, 55
Truffaut, François, 65
Tsubaki Sanjuro, 54
Tsuboi Sakae, 56
Tsuchi, 39
Tsuchi to heitai, 37
Tsuchimoto Noriaki, 74
Tsuji Kichiro, 19f.
Tsukigata Ryunosuke, 21
*tsuma-mono*, 44, 91
Tsuma yo bara no yo ni, 30
*Twenty-four Eyes*, 56

*Twilight Story*, 58
*Typhoon Club*, 83f

Uchida Tomu, 32f., 39
Ueda Akinori, 49
*Ugetsu*, 49
Ugetsu monogatari, 49
Ukigumo, 52–3
Ukigusa, 50
Ukigusa monogatari, 80
*ukiyo-e*, 58, 75, 91
Umaretta wa mita keredo, 29–30, 32, 81
Umi to dokuyaku, 82
Ushihara Kiyohiko, 25f.
Usuzumi no sakura, 74
*Utamaro and Five Women*, 42
Utamaro o meguru gonin no onna, 42

*Vengeance is Mine*, 72
*Village Teacher, A*, 25
*Violence at Noon*, 68

Wada Natto, 59
Waga seisbun ni kui nashi, 43
Wagahai wa nekko de aru, 59
*Wanderers, The*, 60
*War at Sea from Hawaii to Malaya, The*, 38
*What Made Her Do It?*, 32

*When a Woman Ascends the Stairs*, 52
*Wife, Be Like a Rose*, 30
*Whole Family Works, The*, 38
*Woman in the Dunes*, 74
*Woman of Paris, A*, 18
*Wuthering Heights*, 78

Yabure daiko, 45
*yakuza*, 19, 42, 79, 91
Yamada Isuzu, 45
Yamada Nobuo, 75
Yamada Yoji, 80
Yamamoto Kajiro, 38
Yamanaka Sadao, 20, 26, 34–6, 53f.
Yamazaki Toyoko, 59
Yanagimachi Mitsuo, 81
Yoda Yoshitaka, 28, 49
Yoidore tenshi, 46
Yojimbo, 54
Yoru no tsutzumi, 55
Yoshida Chieo, 3
Yoshida Yoshishige, 74f., 78, 81
Yoshimura Kimisaburo, 26, 38, 43, 54
*Younger Brother*, 59
Yuki yukite shingu, 82
Yukinojo henge, 60
Yume miruyoni nemuritai, 84

Zanjin zamba ken, 21